Mr. and Mrs. Louis Vajda, August 20, 1940

DEAR HUBBY OF MINE

Home Front Wives In World War II

By
Diane Phelps Budden

Diane Phelps Budden

Red Rock Mountain Press

For Mom and Dad—Your beautiful letters and photos tell the home front war wives story with amazing intensity, clarity, and warmth. Through the letters I learned so much more about you as immigrants and wartime parents. I only wish the book could have been completed in your lifetimes so you could have read it too.

Library of Congress Cataloging-in-Publication Data

Budden, Diane Phelps
Dear Hubby of Mine: Home Front Wives in World War II
Includes bibliographic references.
ISBN: 978-0-578-55760-1
1. World War II home front
2. Women and World War II
3. World War II love letters
4. Cleveland (Ohio)—Hungarians
940.548173

First Edition

Most of the war news came from the big cabinet radios that were a fixture in every living room...With so much action on so many fronts and the filter of military censorship, they were only getting the big picture. For long stretches of time they had no idea exactly where their husbands were or how they were doing. There were millions of these young wives, women in their twenties, their lives in a state of suspension as they awaited the return of their husbands, always dreading that the unexpected knock at the door would be a telegram or their minister with news that he wouldn't be coming back.

—*The Greatest Generation,* Tom Brokaw, 1998

Contents

Preface

July 17, 1945

Dearest: Sometimes I miss you so, dear, I just think I can't go on for another day. I go to bed and honestly don't care if I ever wake up again. It gets just too, too hard to go on alone like this….
—Love-Love-Love-Irma

Touching letters written by a loving couple; musty letters that detail past lives—my parents' letters. A housewife and a sailor husband with shared immigrant experiences penned more than 500 letters during World War II, and the letters inform this book. Although research I did at the U.S. National Archives, military libraries, and other sources provide the backdrop for this story, I would not have been able to tell it without the letters. I was lucky my parents lived long lives because I was able to ask questions (although not nearly as many as I should have), ferret out details, and fact-check what I had heard over the years. Like many children, I became more interested in my parents' experiences as they aged.

The letters provide a narrative of my parents' lives during wartime. Using abridged versions of the letters I was able to weave a loving romantic story with actual events occurring on the home front and the battlefront. The letters are also brought to life through original family photographs and remembrances. To easily distinguish between the letters of Lou and Irma, his letters are printed in italics, hers in bolded italics. I sometimes used portions of the letters as dialogue, augmenting the conversations and experiences I recall.

While many readers may see the story as a touching romance, and it is, others may appreciate the depiction of the country in the 1940s under wartime conditions and how that culture influenced America in the decades to come. Women charted new roles during the war that led to new freedoms in the 1960s. My parents' immigrant experiences shed light on the experiences of other minority groups and refugees that came before and after them.

The 75th anniversary of the end of World War II is celebrated in 2020. Like my parents, many of the participants have passed on. While servicemen's stories have been broadly told, the tales of the resolute war wives, who had a significant impact on the outcome of the war and the well-being of the country, have not been widely shared. While some women joined the military, and others entered the workforce for the first time, the majority stayed at home to raise children. *Dear Hubby of Mine* focuses on this latter group of women whose stories have been under-represented and largely uncelebrated in World War II literature.

Heroines of the home front, this is your story.

Introduction

January 23, 1944

Dearest Lou: When you left at the station last week Sunday, I had a little idea in the back of my mind that you'd probably be stationed somewhere close enough to come home over weekends. It really never entered my mind that it would be the last time I would see you for a long time. Please say it's not so. I just can't bear to think of you so far away and maybe going farther.

The coming of the new baby is so close now. It will keep me busy fixing the clothes, so will have little time for tears. Lola Lee kept looking for you in the bed in the morning. Then would say, "Daddy all gone" and I would show her your picture and she would say "Love Daddy." And honestly, hon, she hugs the picture and kisses your face.

Will write more tomorrow, dear hubby of mine. I hope I get a letter from you soon. Meantime we all send our love and kisses, oodles and oodles of them.

—Irma & Lola Lee

When I was about ten years old and playing in the dank cellar of our house one summer day, I came upon a few boxes of letters shelved in the old coal bin. I recognized my mother's handwriting on the envelopes: Louis S. Vajda, USS *Bull* APD-78, Fleet Post Office, San Francisco, California. Other letters were addressed to Mrs. Louis Vajda, 2409 Central Avenue, Cleveland,

Ohio. Grabbing some letters, I ran upstairs to the kitchen (smelling deliciously of chocolate chip cookies—my favorite) and yelled to my mother "Can I open these? Can I read them?"

My mother came to the top of the stairs, wiping her hands on her apron. "What do you have, Diane?" she said. I waved the letters over my head. She quickly reached out and took them. "These are private, Diane. They weren't meant for you to read." She looked at me with her stern face—end of conversation.

I questioned my mother about the letters many times. They were letters my parents had exchanged during World War II when my dad was overseas serving in the U.S. Navy. I wondered why they had to be hidden away in the cellar. I was tantalized by what I couldn't have.

Years later, when my mother was almost 95 years old and both her sight and hearing were failing, I was helping her sort through her things for a move to an assisted living facility when I rediscovered the letters. Imagine my surprise when I asked to have them and she replied "Read them if you want to. I don't care anymore."

"Mom, I'm going to write a book with these letters," I said as I gathered them together, so happy to be able to read them.

Her belongings were scattered around the living room of her apartment, some in the yes-it's-going pile, others to be sold, but the bulk earmarked for the local Goodwill store. We both knew that moving to assisted living marked the beginning of a not-so-happy phase of her life, one my father had experienced ten years earlier before he had passed away. She was trying to put a brave face on it.

"That's nice, Diane," she said. "I don't think anyone will care about these old letters but you."

Love letters—a dated concept if ever there is one in this age of smartphones, tablets, and the Internet. My parents exchanged more than 500 letters, plus assorted telegrams, greeting cards, and postcards between 1943 and 1945 that provide an intimate portrait of their lives during World War II. The letters were the lifeline between husband and wife separated during wartime. My father wrote from a battlefront difficult to talk about because of military censors checking for sensitive information; my mother, on the home front in Cleveland, was struggling to understand what was happening and to raise the children alone.

In those days letters were the predominant means of communication when servicemen were overseas, and wives and husbands waited anxiously for them: the heightened anticipation and excitement of a letter matched by the disappointment of one not received. Some letters between servicemen and their wives were lost, discarded, or destroyed to preserve privacy. Irma and Lou saved most of their letters. Lou stored them in his seabag onboard ship and brought them safely home across more than 7,000 miles of blue Pacific Ocean—quite a feat in the midst of a world war.

As a child, these letters piqued my curiosity about what my parents could have written so long ago. I don't know how old I was when I finally realized these were "love letters," and I found it hard to associate such a thing with my parents. I was intrigued by the fact that my mother had saved the letters for so long, bringing them with her wherever she lived. She didn't seem to read them anymore and wouldn't let me read them—until now.

The story of my parents and their letters is also the story of approximately 4 million or more World War II wives whose husbands were in the armed forces, and their estimated 2 million or more children. Some women—approximately 350,000—joined the military. Many women found jobs outside the home, the majority for the first time.

Rosie the Riveter became the icon for women who worked in factories manufacturing war materials while the men were serving in the military. Little did they know they would make history as a bellwether for women who wanted to continue to work outside the home after a taste of independence. They would prefigure the launch of the feminist movement in the late 1960s. Although deserving of admiration as women who broke down barriers in the workforce, they were not typical of the majority of women who were war wives. Seventy-five percent of married women during the war stayed home to raise children. They may not have had adequate family support for their children or they faced their community's negative attitudes about women working versus fulfilling traditional family roles. This book focuses on war wives who were primarily homemakers.

"Oh, I was just a housewife during the war" countless women answered when asked to describe their wartime lives. Home front wives with children were attempting to act as both mother *and* father while shouldering responsibilities of running the household and living with the fear of losing a husband.

Letters, crucial to the well-being of the marriage, flowed back and forth around the world as couples attempted to hold on to the life they shared before the war. What was it like on the home front in wartime America? How did Irma and Lou cope with being separated? How did being a war wife change Irma's life forever?

Chapter 1

An Immigrant Girl Grows Up in the Great Depression

As a young girl, Irma loved to read fairy tales by Hans Christian Andersen and the Brothers Grimm. She was a voracious reader, hiding away in the house and reading every chance she had.

"I believed in all that romance and ever-lasting love between prince and princess, and dreamed I would experience it when I married," she said years later. "I was so silly!"

Books could have helped her to face the stresses her family was under during the Great Depression and to straddle the two worlds she lived in. Growing up in the 1920s in a Hungarian community in Cleveland, Ohio, Irma experienced the unsettling differences in lifestyle between her immigrant family and the world outside their neighborhood. Immigrant groups coming to America lived among their own kind, especially Eastern Europeans who were part of the last great wave of immigrants in the early 1900s and were often considered culturally inferior by their adopted country.

"I remember running home from school one day with my books, while boys yelling 'Hunky! Hunky!' chased after me," said Irma. The incident brought back unpleasant memories.

Irma's parents had emigrated from Hungary: Charles Bodnar in 1907, when he was 16, and Lila Nagy in May 1914, when she was 22. They had been part of an unprecedented mass migration of Eastern and Southern Europeans to America between 1880 and

1920. The 1920 U.S. Census counted almost 1 million people either born in Hungary or having Hungarian-born parents. Cleveland had the largest population of Hungarians in the country and earned the nickname "Little Budapest."

Lila had never traveled very far from Szabed, Hungary, the small peasant village in the Transylvania area where she was born, but she probably was encouraged to make the voyage by her sister Agnes who already lived in the United States. Lila and other immigrants were seeking a new life in a country believed to have boundless economic opportunities. Coming to America gave them a chance to work hard and better themselves. World War I, the Great War, began in July 1914, so Lila barely escaped further hardships in Hungary, which may have been the catalyst for her voyage.

Getting to her new country was a lengthy voyage of seven to ten days across an often rough and stormy ocean. She was traveling with her cousin Anne to Cleveland, where family had settled. They shared space in steerage class on the ocean liner USS *Carpathia* with 1,140 other immigrants. They couldn't afford a first- or second-class cabin. (Steerage tickets cost approximately $30). They each had an iron bunk bed with a straw mattress and shared the few available bathrooms. Topside there was only a small deck area, so most passengers chose to remain in the crowded steerage compartment for most of the trip to tend to their seasickness.

When the ship sailed into New York harbor, what could the unsophisticated young woman from the farm have thought? She knew about the Statue of Liberty that greeted all newcomers from earlier emigrants who had traveled the same path. Did it make her feel welcome? Everything, starting with the vast Manhattan skyline, would have been so foreign compared to her homeland and her small village.

After being processed by an immigration officer on Ellis Island, Lila was ferried ashore to where her sister Agnes waited. They hugged and chatted excitedly in Hungarian while other immigrants around them greeted family in myriad languages.

Lila stayed with her sister for a short time before traveling to Cleveland to live with an aunt in the westside Hungarian neighborhood. Both the Buckeye Avenue neighborhood on the east side, and the smaller westside Lorain Avenue neighborhood were very welcoming to Hungarian immigrants. The new arrivals were glad to be among fellow countrymen who provided help with housing and finding jobs and allayed their fears about their strange new country.

Wedding photo of Mr. and Mrs. Charles Bodnar. (1915)

In 1915, Lila met and married another Hungarian immigrant, Charles Bodnar. Lila's wedding portrait pictured a tiny girlish woman with a very serious expression for such a happy occasion. The couple posed in front of a staged backdrop supplied by the photographer, along with a flower stand overflowing with white carnations made of cloth. Lila's traditional lacy white dress and headpiece with perky flowers and trailing veil were probably borrowed or maybe rented. Charles was dressed in a black suit with a white shirt, bowtie, and gloves, and he looked very handsome with his hair slicked back in an impressive wavy pompadour. He wore a leafy boutonniere. The oval photo was encircled with a border of flowers and printed on a round aluminum disc, a novel framing choice at the time.

Irma, their first child, was born on June 20, 1916, in the family apartment with the help of a midwife. Her birth certificate stated her name as Olga Bodnar. While she was growing up, Irma lobbied to have her first name changed to Irma, and Olga became her middle name, very unusual because Hungarians in the "old country" didn't give middle names to their children. Irma must have wanted to follow the traditions of their new country. She never really liked the name Olga, so she rarely used it.

Irma with her mother and father, Lila and Charles Bodnar. (1919)

In a photo of her at perhaps a year old, Irma was dressed in a coat with a fur collar and matching muff. She had inherited her mother's frizzy, unruly hair, a challenge to contain and style. In a family photo taken when she was about three years old Irma stands as instructed, looking at the camera in her little white dress with bows sewn around the waist. Sometime later, she posed in a gypsy costume for a dance recital, looking very pleased as she extended her hand to her partner.

"I liked my dance classes," she said. "We learned Hungarian folk dances too."

Irma and her family moved frequently, always settling in the Lorain Avenue Hungarian neighborhood. Lila and Charles worked in various factories, and the family struggled to make a living. A son, Charles Jr., was born in 1921.

At one point Lila owned a beauty salon. She was a self-taught hairdresser, wielding a two-pronged metal curler heated on the stovetop to style hair for neighborhood women. "Ear-ma" (as her mother called her, maybe a result of her Hungarian accent) needed to help in the store after school or babysit her brother.

Eventually, they opened a secondhand furniture store, and the family lived in an apartment above the shop. The family couldn't survive economically without Lila working in various family businesses or local factories. Some women managed boardinghouses for immigrant men, "birds of passage," as they worked and saved money to return to the old country. Now and then Lila had boarders who rented one of the bedrooms in their home.

Irma and her brother soon found that Eastern European immigrants were not especially welcome in the crowded city outside their neighborhood where housing and jobs were scarce. In spite of the stark contrasts between her neighborhood and the outside world, and the prejudices endured, Irma had a fierce desire to fit in and "be American." Her mother never fully mastered the language, and spoke broken English all her life. Because neither of her parents could read English, Irma served as interpreter and go-between with the outside world, and she learned to balance and live in both worlds, as children of immigrants often do.

When Irma's family moved to another westside apartment in Cleveland, her parents joined one of the many Hungarian social clubs in the neighborhood to visit with Hungarian friends. The women organized potlucks on the weekends, making favorite Hungarian dishes like stuffed cabbage with sauerkraut, apple strudel, and fried doughnuts. Bingo was a popular activity among the women. Although Lila was not a gambler, she loved to play bingo with Irma by her side translating the English. They shared the excitement of possibly winning a prize. The women also had card parties, using the deck from the old country with Hungarian images and words.

The club was the center of many community events—wedding receptions, anniversary celebrations, and the annual Grape Festival. The Grape Festival had peasant roots in Hungary as a celebration for the successful harvest season. At the Hungarian hall, children dressed in traditional Hungarian costumes performed typical folk dances from the old country, and Irma joined in.

Before the folk dancing and soulful violin gypsy music began at the festival, and following a custom hundreds of years old, club members attached clusters of grapes to rope strung high in the hall's side yard, a veritable cloud of red and purple overhead. Children, and even some mischievous adults, would try to "steal" the grapes without being caught by the "judge," who fined the thieves while embarrassing them as loudly as possible. Irma's mother, usually quiet and reserved, plucked grapes that were out of Irma's reach, and barely within her own, as fast as possible. As they made off with their grapes, Lila would yell encouragement to other would-be thieves.

Irma's father had a formidable personality and ran a tight, paternalistic ship. He always wore a suit and tie and fedora in the city, adding to an austere demeanor not given to smiling and laughing. He was an accomplished player of Hungarian folk songs on the traditional cimbalom, a trapezoidal-shaped stringed instrument beaten with a set of small wooden hammers, and often played at the club.

The whole family catered to his moods and loud outbursts, and someone would eventually become the object of his threatening yells. Irma was a bit afraid of him. Too often his volatile temper and sharp tongue were directed at her.

"He criticized everything I did," she said years later. His words stung, and she carried the baggage of hurtful comments all her life. Irma's mother often tried to redirect his anger, quietly begging him to calm down.

When Irma was a young teen, her parents bought a small farmhouse in the Cleveland countryside that enabled them to plant a small garden and raise chickens and geese, just as they had in Hungary. The goose feathers were used to make fluffy feather pillows and comforters covered with handmade duvets. The goose fat was rendered to make soap.

"I was afraid of those geese and ran away from them as fast as I could," said Irma. "They would chase me around and snap at my heels."

Irma's family hosted many picnics for family and friends from the city during this time, happy for the warm camaraderie and the opportunity to share Hungarian meals together.

In the summer mother and daughter rented a stand in the outdoor arcade at the downtown West Side Market to sell vegetables and eggs from the farm. The fragrant smell of her mother's dill weed blended with the other earthy aromas in the air. The market was crowded with immigrant vendors and shoppers of many different nationalities looking for ingredients for ethnic dishes. There were opportunities to visit with like-minded Hungarian friends and to buy or barter farm-fresh foods for supper. Late in the afternoon as the yellow-brick clock tower chimed the hour, they would ride home on the streetcar with all their bundles.

Irma's generation was part of a new teen culture in the United States that developed during the 1920s and 1930s. Influenced by mass communications, like music and movies, the culture was also fostered by the expansion of public schools as parents increasingly realized the importance of education if their children were to do better than they had. Schooling eventually led to age segregation and high schools, which allowed teens to develop their own identity and to socialize away from the watchful eyes of their parents.

While attending school, Irma developed an interest in clothing design, especially after visiting her Aunt Agnes in New York City. She had already begun making clothes for herself, even though she yearned for a store-bought dress like other girls outside the neighborhood were wearing. She struggled to control her weight and attempted to sew clothes that complimented her figure. Teens in the 1930s styled their hair in tightly permed waves, and Irma followed the trend, sweeping her dark brown hair back from her forehead. Eyebrows were penciled-in lines, much like those of the movie stars they admired.

In 1932 in her junior year Irma enrolled in a local school in Cleveland, the Darvas School of Fashion Arts. The school had been founded in 1910 to provide classes in household skills. In 1932 it launched the Darvas Fashion Service Program for "girls and women who are artistically inclined, and enjoy clothes that enhance personality for themselves and for others." Courses were offered in fashion sketching, costume design, dressmaking, and millinery (hatmaking).

Darvas Fashion School advertisement,
The Cleveland Plain Dealer (1932)

The schooling would have been an additional financial strain on the family during the Great Depression, but Irma's mother supported her career choice. It probably helped that the founders and many of the students were Hungarian. Irma was glad to be at Darvas instead of the local high school.

In order to graduate, Irma had to design and sew a dress, and model it at the graduation ceremonies held at the grand Hotel Winton downtown. She made a green cotton pique dress with a brown organdy apron, perhaps influenced by the popularity of the apron dress designed by famed Italian designer Elsa Schiaparelli. The school was so impressed with Irma's dress that they asked to keep it as part of their teaching library for future students.

"I was considered a star student," she said, proudly.

Irma graduates from Darvas Fashion School. (1934)

Irma earned her diploma at Darvas Fashion Arts in the spring of 1934 and sported a class ring that her mother would have been hard pressed to afford. In her graduation photo, her serious expression reflects the importance she and her family placed on the day.

Irma passed her autograph book around to her friends during the years she was in school. Many wrote in Hungarian. Among them was a group of best friends that called themselves the "Jolly-eight," and they wrote heartfelt wishes for the future. Alice, on June 14, 1932, wrote:

Dear Irma:

May your joys be as deep as the ocean, and your sorrows light as foam.

Helen, another friend among the Jolly-eight wrote on June 18,1932:

In the golden chain of friendship, regard me as a link.

Mary wrote on December 14, 1934:

When rocks and hills divide us
And you are far away,
Remember it was one of the
Jolly-Eight girls
That wrote to you today!
P.S. Hope you have triplets—all girls!

A sober message from one of Irma's instructors at the school reflected the unfolding economic calamity in the country:

Set your goal—
You'll get there—
Fight for it—Your instructor, Miss Leone

Miss Leone's advice indicated the difficulties of finding a suitable job in 1934, when one-third of Cleveland workers were unemployed. Irma was 18 years old, and her family, like others, was suffering from the effects of the Great Depression when jobs of any kind were hard to come by and incomes had plunged.

In 1935 Irma visited her Aunt Agnes in New York City, hopeful that her dressmaking skills would be employable there. When a job didn't materialize, she returned to Cleveland and worked for a tailor, then a milliner, and for a dress shop making alterations for customers. She might have liked to work for one of the large department stores in downtown Cleveland, but perhaps her experience (and confidence) weren't sufficient to land a job.

Irma used her clever and impressive design and seamstress skills to fashion clothing for herself that reflected popular styles. Using patterns from the Butterick and McCall companies, she sewed clothes in the latest styles, using whatever fabrics were available during the Great Depression. She often had to make clothes by reusing fabric from an outdated article of clothing.

Like millions of other Americans in the late 1930s, Irma was an ardent movie fan.

She bought movie magazines like *Modern Screen* and *Photoplay* from the newsstand and studied the latest film fashions. She also enjoyed other magazines, like the new *Woman's Day* available at the grocery store. She and her girlfriends followed the popular movie stars of the day, admiring the beautiful clothes they wore both onscreen and off and mimicking their hairstyles.

"We loved going to the movies," said Irma. "Clark Gable movies were our favorite." She and her girlfriends also dressed up and went to dances in town to listen to the Big Band songs of the day.

"Our favorite crooners were Bing Crosby and Frank Sinatra," she said. "I was not very sophisticated, but I was proud. I didn't have any boyfriends or even date, but enjoyed the company of my girlfriends."

The friends also donned slacks and with their pant legs rolled up went bike riding or waded in streams near the farm. This might have been a bit daring for the 1930s. It wasn't until World War II that wearing pants became more acceptable for women, although casual styles were gaining in popularity for both men and women.

Irma and her friends bike near the farm. (1934)

Irma and her friends volunteered at the West Side Community House in 1937. She helped out with the girls club or the popular daycare program for babies and children. The organization was founded as a settlement house in 1890 by the Methodist Episcopal Church. Over the years it became a center for community services and activities for immigrant children and their families, assisting them in the Americanization process by offering classes in English, citizenship, and American customs and traditions.

Irma and her friends volunteer at the local Community House. (1937)

As the summer of 1939 began to fade, Irma and her girlfriends attended the National Air Races at Cleveland Hopkins Airport, home to the popular event for many years in spite of the Depression. At a few of the previous events, Charles Lindbergh performed, and Amelia Earhart competed. The airplane races provided a few bold women an opportunity to showcase their pilot skills, demonstrating that women could match the men. For some women it led to organizing transcontinental flights (including Earhart's fatal around-the-world trip in 1937). The 1939 Air Races were the last ones held until after World War II.

Meanwhile in Europe, Hitler had invaded Poland, marking the beginning of World War II and heralding a sea change in the lives of all Americans.

Chapter 2

The Newlyweds

Irma loved going to the annual Hungarian Grape Festival at the neighborhood social hall. Watching the colorful folk dance troupe brought back memories of her years performing with the group. Everyone grabbed a cluster or two of purple grapes strung up in the courtyard, laughing and shrieking, enjoying this old tradition.

As usual, she had come with her parents, who were whirling around the dance floor with the other adults, hands on each other's shoulders. They were dancing the familiar Hungarian *Csárdás* accompanied by violins and a stringed cimbalom.

Irma was secretly hoping she might find some new friends. Maybe a boyfriend? *It's 1938 and I'm 22 years old,* she thought. *I'm living with my parents with no marriage prospects. The guy I met in New York City while living with my aunt and working at Tiffany's wasn't the right one. I'm ready to get on with my life. Ma knows a man she wants me to meet.*

She looked around the room for her girlfriends. She wanted them to see her new dress. She had remade an outdated frock into a popular style, and bought a matching belt and new shoes. Ma had fixed her hair. *I probably don't look as pretty as the other girls,* she thought. She had seen a lot of single men in the hall, maybe they would ask her to dance.

Her mother suddenly appeared at her side. "Irma," she said, "I want you to meet the son of a friend of mine. His name is Louis Vajda."

"Hello, Irma," he said, stammering a bit. "Everyone calls me Lou. Would you like to dance?"

"Yes, I would," she said. Her dark eyes sparkled and a smile lit up her face, like she was contemplating an exciting adventure.

Louis Vajda was born in Budapest, Hungary on October 24, 1913, soon after the start of World War I in Europe. His family emigrated from Hungary, on April 30, 1921. Louis was 7, his brother John was 9, and his half-sister Margaret was 13. His name was listed on the passenger ship manifest as Lasslo (maybe a misspelling of Laszlo) Vajda.

"I had to leave my little red wagon behind," Lou said many years later with uncharacteristic emotion. "And I never got a new one. My family didn't have the money." This was Lou's strongest memory of his family's emigration—the loss of his little red wagon.

While he was growing up his family changed his name to Louis, maybe in honor of his Uncle Louis and probably to give him a more acceptable American name. He gained a middle name too, Steve, perhaps in honor of another relative or family friend. His family had chosen to live in Cleveland near his father's brother Louis, who had sponsored them. Uncle Louis had found his father a job with the Otis Steel Company, as well as a place for the family to live in the westside Lorain Avenue neighborhood.

Both Louie and his brother Johnny had typical *Magyar* (ethnic Hungarian) features—dark brown eyes and thick wavy hair, olive complexions, and short, slight builds. Johnny was more outgoing and self-confident than Lou, but they were both fun-loving and carefree by nature. Their older sister Margaret suffered the painful experience of starting school in Cleveland as a teen without knowing English. She was the only one of the three siblings who spoke English with a distinct accent.

Lou's family was lucky that they immigrated before the United States enacted the Immigration Law of 1921 that instituted new restrictions that favored Northern Europeans. The law set annual quotas by nationality to 3 percent of their number in the country in the 1910 census. It limited Eastern Europeans to roughly 175,000 individuals who could still enter "the golden doors" of America. When the "huddled masses yearning to breathe free" arrived in New York harbor, they soon learned that the famous poem by Emma Lazarus inscribed on the base of the Statue of Liberty didn't really express the country's feelings about immigration at the time.

A law passed in 1924 reduced quotas further, and in 1927 the number of individuals who could enter the country was capped at 150,000 individuals. Yearly quotas for Hungarians dropped to 869 people. This proved to be a hardship for Hungarians settled in the United States, because they lost the ability to help relatives immigrate from the old country. Eventually, they were cut off from their roots.

Lou dropped out of Orchard High School after the ninth grade when he was 16 years old, probably because his family needed him to help with household expenses. He wasn't a very good student, but he could read and write English. He eventually forgot how to write Hungarian.

His first job was as a mover on a furniture store truck. A year later he found a job at Cleveland's largest commercial bakery, Rosen's Bakery, where he made, baked, and packaged sweet rolls and other pastries on the night shift. Like other bakery employees, Lou also worked part-time at Laub's or Spang Bakery, depending on their production needs. He couldn't seem to find a satisfying direction in life, and was limited by his lack of education and job experience. It likely didn't help that he was an Eastern European immigrant. He applied to become a citizen in April 1936 and became a naturalized citizen in September 1939.

Although Lou wasn't an overly ambitious man, he had noticed that everybody else his age seemed to be moving ahead. His sister Margaret was married and had a daughter Jeanne, while he was still living at home with his parents and Johnny, who also hadn't found a job to his liking. Margaret knew Lou was restless and unhappy with his various jobs. He and Johnny also liked to party with friends a bit too much. Lou's family hoped he would soon find employment that would support him, and maybe a wife and child too.

"You're not a young man anymore," his sister reminded him.

Lou was a bit vain about his appearance and took pains to comb the waves in his hair back from his forehead, slicking them down with hair lotion. He always had a well-trimmed moustache, and his close shave was powdered with Mennen's aftershave talc powder.

Although he considered himself good-looking, Lou didn't have anyone special in his life, perhaps because he had so little money. But he was also an introvert and socially awkward, so he was not adept at small talk. When he was nervous or put on the spot, he stammered a bit.

His wardrobe was limited, but he had a good suit, which he usually accessorized with a fedora. Fedoras were made popular by Hollywood films of the '30s, worn by sinister gangsters like Edward G. Robinson and James Cagney in *Public Enemy* and Paul Muni in *Scarface*. Lou was fond of fedoras. The wide brim could be snapped into a number of shapes, but commonly the brim was pulled down in the front and slanted to the right side of the head. It could hide the protruding ears he thought detracted from his good looks. He took a lot of kidding about his ears.

Louis didn't get angry very often, but could be difficult if something set him off, especially if he was drinking. Like all the men in his family, he smoked Chesterfield cigarettes, especially in social situations. He had a stubborn streak that could cause friction with others in the family, but he was generally easygoing. Hungarian families tended to be very talkative and emotional in expressing themselves, using their arms and hands to get a point across. Everyone spoke louder and more rapidly to make their point. Lou's voice could get lost in the uproar.

Lou wearing his favorite fedora. (1927)

He joined the Rosen Bakery Local 19 baseball league and played for a few years, even though he didn't follow the Cleveland Indians, the professional team in town, or other sports teams. He enjoyed going out after the games with his teammates to a local bar for beers and camaraderie. For the same reason, he joined a bowling league and played weekly.

At the time Irma met Lou, she was living with her parents. When her family was counted in the 1940 federal census, they were renting an apartment in the Lorain Avenue neighborhood and spending summer weekends at the farm. Her father was a machinist and claimed to be making $660 in 1939; he had been unemployed during some part of the year. Her mother was listed as a baker at the Spang Baking Company, making $664. Irma was working as a dressmaker with an income of $936; her brother, Chuck, had just graduated from high school

On the 1940 federal census, Lou reported income for 1939 as $1,300. He was working as a baker's helper at Laub's Baking Company, located in a busy retail area on Lorain Avenue. His job description said he was "experienced on all bakery goods manufacturing jobs." He still lived at home with his parents and brother, John, in the Lorain Avenue area of Cleveland. Most immigrants lived close to where they worked so they could walk or ride the streetcar to their jobs, because most did not own automobiles.

When Irma and Lou began dating, they often double-dated with his brother, Johnny, and his girlfriend, often ending up at the farm. Irma's mother made them a nice supper of their favorite Hungarian dishes.

"That Johnny was a kidder," said Irma. "I liked him real well."

All of Irma's girlfriends thought Lou was very handsome with his dark ruddy complexion and deep brown eyes. Like many other Hungarian men, he always sported a trim moustache that framed his upper lip and fanned out when he smiled.

"Wow, Lou is sure good-looking," Irma's friend Rose told her. "I love his moustache."

A fond memory that both of them would recall in their war letters were the times when Lou borrowed his father's car and they drove around town at night.

"Lou would bring warm cinnamon rolls to my house after work," Irma said. "I filled a thermos bottle with hot coffee, and we would drive to Edgewater Park on Lake Erie to enjoy the city lights with our coffee and rolls. We talked about our day and our future together." The smell of cinnamon rolls and coffee stayed with her all her life as a remembrance of happy times before the war started.

Irma and Lou, like many other Americans, were avid movie fans. They took the streetcar downtown to the movie theaters to see the double feature with cartoons and newsreels. The newsreels showed the battles and civilian turmoil of the war in Europe and Japan. By 1940 movie attendance had increased to 80 million a week, tickets cost 24 cents, and *Grapes of Wrath* was named Best Picture of the Year.

They occasionally went out to dinner in downtown Cleveland. For one special celebration they had dinner at the popular Alpine Village supper club, "Cleveland's Theatre Restaurant," complete with a glitzy chorus line of dancing girls and big-name entertainers and celebrities. They ordered Manhattans and toasted the night away, Irma feeling very hoity-toity and entranced with the romantic evening.

They and some friends drove out to Euclid Beach Amusement Park on the shores of Lake Erie.

"It was so much fun," said Irma. "We rode the Bug and Rocket Ships. The Laff in the Dark ride was a little scary. I was glad to have Lou hold me tight."

They brought a picnic and found a table near the large Art Deco-designed dance pavilion to talk and eat.

"After supper, we danced all night under the twinkling lights," said Irma, her eyes sparkling.

Lou and Irma celebrate their engagement. (1940)

Irma and Lou were married on August 17, 1940, by a pastor at St. John's Evangelical Church in downtown Cleveland. It was not the family's place of worship; in fact, Irma's family did not attend church or practice Catholicism as many other Hungarians did.

They exchanged a tender kiss—Lou was very affectionate. Irma's maid of honor was her friend Viola Pink; the best man was her brother Chuck. For her wedding attire, Irma made a flattering pale pink lightweight wool dress and matching jacket with a faux fur collar. She had chosen a plain wedding band to match her engagement ring that had a small round diamond surrounded by diamond chips. Lou didn't want a ring.

"Hon, I won't wear it," he said.

"I want all the other girls to know you are mine," she replied.

The wedding photo shows a happy couple: Lou with his trademark moustache above a warm smile and a white rose boutonniere; Irma with her tightly waved hair and a white orchid corsage on her lapel. She liked the delicate beauty of orchids.

Lou and Irma held their wedding reception at her parents' farm. The few guests were seated picnic-style at an outdoor table. They served typical Hungarian dishes: stuffed cabbage, chicken paprika, apple strudel, poppy seed rolls, and *Dobos Torta*, Irma's favorite

Hungarian cake. Lou's sister was supposed to bring the traditional wedding cake.

Lou and Irma's wedding reception at the farm. (1940)

"Margaret forgot to buy it," said Irma. It was a lifelong regret: a wedding without a wedding cake. There was so little money for the wedding of her dreams—a middle-class American wedding as portrayed in the magazines she read—that for years she harbored resentment toward Margaret about the cake.

"I think she neglected to bring it on purpose," she often said.

The newlyweds went to New York City for their honeymoon, taking many tours of the city's points of interest. While visiting the Statue of Liberty, Irma purchased a small copper replica of the statue. They kept a list of their expenses in a little notebook. The highlight of the trip was a visit to the New York World's Fair.

"It was a dream come true for me," she said. "There were all kinds of modern designs for houses, furniture, and clothing. Lou was excited to see the new automobile models."

The economic disaster of the 1930s had brought food shortages and massive unemployment that had lingered into the '40s. Everyone was ready to focus on a future that would surely be more promising. Ironically, the 1940 World Fair's theme was "For Peace and Freedom" and celebrated international cooperation.

The fair covered more than 1200 acres outside New York City. Sixty countries were represented, as well as 33 states. Many large corporations had exhibits: Coca-Cola, IBM, Ford, Chrysler Motors, General Motors, Eastman Kodak, to name a few. The new discipline of industrial design introduced the country to the revolutionary Modernistic style popular in Europe: streamlined, simple designs for work and home in place of the overdone decorative look of the 1920s. Robotics, television, FM radio, and fluorescent lighting were displayed for the first time at the fair. The automobile exhibit dominated the space as automakers marketed to a ready audience. The fair would prove to have a lasting effect on American design ideals, culture, and consumerism.

The couple stayed with her Aunt Agnes in New York City and took the subway to the fair for 5 cents. They attended on August 22, 1940, at a cost of 50 cents each. Given her dressmaking skills Irma was delighted to visit the World of Fashion pavilion to view the R. H. Macy style show. According to the *Official Guide Book of the World's Fair,* "The World of Fashion is out to prove that American styles for American women have come into their own to stay." There were exhibits about new textiles; a Parade of Labels exhibit featured creations by top fashion designers; and other areas presented the newest footwear, undergarments, cosmetics, and hats.

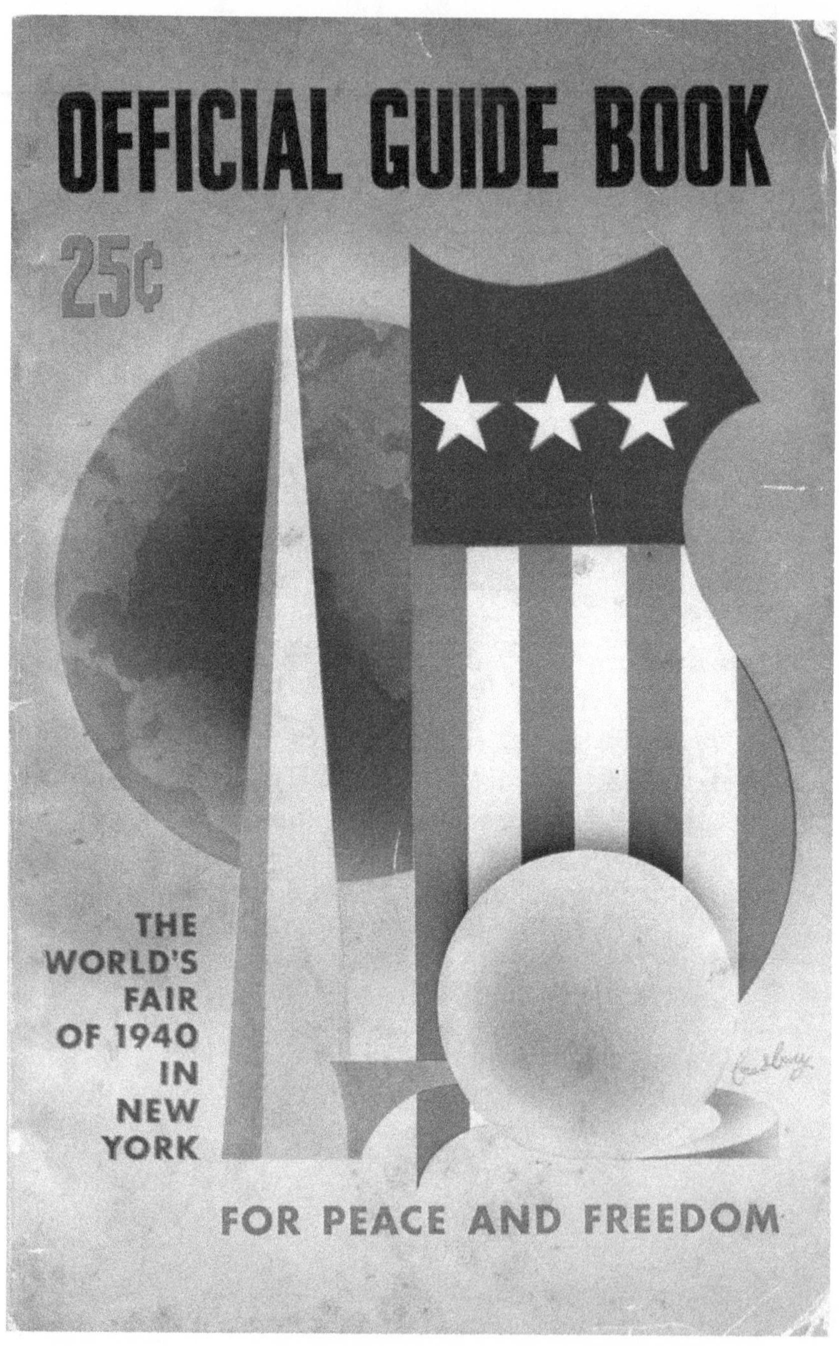

1940 World's Fair Program

WORLD'S FAIR DAILY

5¢ 5¢

Published Daily by Rogers-Kellogg-Stillson, Inc., 461 8th Ave., New York
Editorial and Advertising Offices: BRyant 9-5000

No. 104 Thursday, August 22, 1940

Visitors To See Dive Bomber In Action

Firestone Stages Safari

What is believed to be the first public demonstration of a terminal velocity dive by one of the latest type export bombers developed by the Republic Aircraft Corporation is scheduled this afternoon over the Fair grounds if the proposed demonstration receives the approval of the Civil Aeronautics Authority.

The bomber, which attains an ordinary cruising speed of 350 miles an hour, will climb to approximately 12,000 feet and make the dive at a speed between 600 and 700 miles per hour, pulling out about 3,000 feet above the Fair.

Aviation also is the keynote of the Good Neighbor Broadcast to Chile originating at Inter-America House at 8 P.M. R. H. Welch, vice-president and general manager of the Bendix Aviation Company, will recount the part aviation has played in the development of Chile, "a treasure house of the Western world". The broadcast will be carried to South America by CBS short wave.

A colorful safari, headed by an elephant carrying a howdah in which will ride company officials, hammock bearers and outriders on horses, from the LIRR ramp to the Firestone exhibit will mark the opening ceremonies of Firestone Southeast Contest Winners Day. Participants in the safari are winners of a Firestone sales contest held throughout the southeastern part of the country. The visitors will be entertained at luncheon at the Ford and Firestone buildings after which they will tour the grounds by tractor train.

Gold from Flushing's newly discovered "gold mine" is on display at Gimbel Town for a period of two weeks. Next Sunday "Prospector" Violet Klemovish, the scrub woman, who discovered the gold, assayed at $19.20 per ton, in the subsoil of her cellar at 136-52 Thirty-Seventh Ave., and her family, will be guests at Gimbel Town.

The Brazilian Pavilion opens a new coffee exhibit today which shows fifteen different grades, achieved by variations in curing and roasting, of one type of coffee. Visitors will have an opportunity of tasting the flavor of the different grades at the coffee bar.

TURN TO 'SPECIAL EVENTS' FOR TIME SCHEDULES

1940 World's Fair Newsletter

They ate lunch at the Hungary pavilion where goulash was available for 35 cents or they could purchase a complete meal for 95 cents. Irma bought a bookmark with red wooden dancing boots attached, and a small ceramic blue-and-white folk pitcher and plate from Hungary. She visited the American Art Today galleries where artists demonstrated their skills. Printmakers were using lithography or etching presses to make prints.

Irma bought a modern print at the fair for her home. In shades of ivory, sage green, and pale yellow, the signed print featured a serpentine couple intertwined and rising at sunrise from the center of a flower blossom. It was one in a series depicting dawn, midday, and dusk in the Art Deco style. The sensual piece idealized love and the romantic feelings of a couple newly married. She hung it over their bed.

When Irma and Lou returned home from New York, Irma compiled a scrapbook of the wedding and the honeymoon with their corsages pressed between the pages. It displayed greeting cards from their friends and postcards they had bought at New York City attractions. It was filled with romantic souvenirs.

The couple lived with her parents until they could afford an apartment of their own. The house was small, especially for newlyweds, and Irma and her father often clashed. She wasn't happy about the arrangement, but what could she do? She was anxious for them to be out on their own.

Raised by immigrant parents during very tough economic times Irma didn't benefit from a stable, middle-class home life. She always felt that her glass was half-empty instead of half-full. "I wasn't very sure of myself," she said.

Irma was extremely sensitive to slights, and it fueled the volatile side of her personality. Much like her father, her temper flared easily during family disagreements. She hoped her marriage would allow her to build a new life that reflected her plans and dreams.

Lou had a very easygoing personality and liked dancing and parties.

"Let's go to the club to dance," he would urge. "Your girlfriends will be there too." She often preferred more solitary pursuits for them, more alone time to talk and plan.

Lou's happy-go-lucky attitude and ready grin contrasted with her desire for stability, and, like her mother, she wasn't quick to smile or laugh. She hesitated to show her feelings until she understood the circumstances and her place in them, so she could appear very tentative and anxious.

Irma felt it was important to follow society's rules to gain entry into the lifestyle and class she coveted. She tried to persuade Lou to embrace her vision of the future, but the only thing he really wanted was a new car. This would eventually create discord between them, but for the most part Lou was looking for direction and a home so he fell into line behind her.

"I'm happy if Irma's happy," he always said.

As 1940 came to a close they celebrated at a New Year's Eve party with friends. She designed and sewed a black silk evening dress. She accessorized the gown with her gold collar necklace and earrings with ruby-colored stones, a Christmas gift from Lou.

"The sequins were sewn over the front of the gown," she said. She made an upward motion with her fingers to illustrate how the sequins sprinkled over the bodice. "Even Margaret asked to borrow it for a party."

Irma and her girlfriends were part of the Friday Night Club that met at local restaurants. Each woman would wear a hat style in vogue: wide-brimmed straw boaters, encircled with tulle or nylon netting and decorated with fabric flowers; upturned flowerpot hats or turbans fashioned of felt; felt berets; pillboxes with feathers and bows; chaplets or curvettes that fit snugly to the head and were adorned with small flowers, feathers, ribbons, sequins, or partial veils covering the eyes. Irma tended to wear curvettes or pillboxes and probably owned only one.

The Friday Night Club (1943)

It was also possible to make attractive hats using Butterick or McCall patterns or to redo a current hat for a new occasion. Irma's millinery class at the Darvas School of Fashion allowed her to design styles as money allowed, although hats became more affordable over the years and cost less than buying or remaking a new dress to refresh her wardrobe.

Like many newlyweds, Lou and Irma would quarrel over differences of opinion on how to spend household money. She bought a new dress that Lou thought was too expensive. They had an angry exchange when she wouldn't return it. She eventually remade it into a new dress.

Irma and her girlfriends chose to wear slacks for activities in the countryside like bike riding, but it wasn't until women began working in factories manufacturing war materials that pants became popular. An April 1, 1942, article in *Vogue* "A Primer on Pants," advised readers: "Today, there are…three kinds of occasions that thoroughly justify, practically demand, slacks. When you're in the country. When you're on war service duty…When you're busy at good hard work...Slacks look wonderfully well when they're right, incredibly bad when they're wrong...If you're in doubt, don't. A skirt is never wrong."

Lou had been working at the bakery for twelve years, only making $32.50 per week. In July 1942, he got a better job at Cleveland Graphite Bronze Company as a furnace operator. With it came a substantial pay increase: Lou was earning $45 per week. When their daughter, Lola Lee was born in September 1942, they moved to a westside apartment of their own. The future they had hoped for, and had been promised by the World's Fair, would not materialize any time soon, but Irma was happy they finally had their own home even if it was only several streets over from her parents' house.

"As soon as we had enough money, I bought new furniture," she said. "We bought a bedroom set, a five-piece credenza, and end tables for the living room. I also had Lou pick out a comfortable chair for himself." The furniture reflected the influence of the modern designs she had seen at the World's Fair. It proved to be timeless, and she moved it from house to house.

They also had enough money to purchase a little tan coupe for Lou to drive to work and take Irma around town and to her Friday Night Club outings. Irma never did get a driver's license.

"I was afraid I would cause an accident and hurt someone," she confessed.

With the bombing of Pearl Harbor on December 7, 1941, America could no longer resist involvement in World War II. Cleveland reacted as much of the country did and began preparing for war. The papers and radio were full of talk about the men marching off to war, and parades were organized when it was time for them to leave for training camps, complete with a small band supplied by the May Company department store. Everyone was abuzz with the explosive changes happening. Movies portrayed men going off to war and the women they left behind. Irma was worried.

"I really am alarmed," she said to her friend, Rose. "Here Lou is toying with joining the Navy and we are in these fierce battles in foreign places with strange-sounding names. I'm scared. He should be too. What would we do if something happened to him? With me expecting again. And he just got a better paying job."

Lou's father worked at the Otis Steel Company. The October 1942 issue of "The Otis Sheet" warehouse newsletter featured Lou and Irma's wedding photo with the caption "A handsome young man, eh, girls?" as well as a photo of Sgt. John Vajda, Jr., Lou's brother, with an appeal to buy war bonds.

The family gathered at the couple's apartment after Lola Lee's christening. Irma's brother, Chuck, who had joined the Navy after the attack on Pearl Harbor in 1941, was home on leave. Her parents came in from the farm, happy to be with their only grandchild. It was a happy time.

The family celebrating Lola Lee's christening. (1942)

With war raging overseas, Irma questioned Lou about his desire to join the Navy. "If you think you need to try this," she told him, "give it a try, I guess. I'm sure you will be stationed somewhere nearby and be able to come home on the weekends. I want to support your choice, but I'm worried for me and the baby too."

It wasn't until he was gone that she understood the real impact his enlistment would have on their family and the challenges she would face as a war wife.

Chapter 3

1943: Boot Camp Blues

Lou had always wanted to be in the Navy, even though his brother-in-law Chuck warned him about Navy life.

"Say hello to my impatient brother-in-law," Chuck wrote in a letter to Irma, "and tell him to stay put. Don't let the movies fool you, Louie, it isn't just a big bowl of cherries. Take it from me you are better off at home, and I'm not kidding.

"You see, I have an idea of where I'm going, and I've talked to fellows that have been there and they don't paint a pretty picture. They're saying they're glad to be back in the states and are willing to stay here. I wish Louie could talk to some of the boys that were lucky enough to come back."

Lou's brother Johnny was in agreement. "I heard Lou's in the Coast Guard Reserves," Johnny wrote. "He always did like the Navy. Hope he does not have to get in this war. Hope to hell it's over soon, and I get home and live like people should. Do your mother and father have that little farm yet? Sure would like to go out to that little farm on Sundays like we used to."

Lou had hoped that Coast Guard training would help him qualify for the Navy. Lou joined the U.S. Coast Guard in January 1943 to augment his income, which would help with the expenses of a new baby. He was in training for six months and then served in temporary reserves on patrol duty. During that time, he had a bald eagle from the seal of the U.S. Navy tattooed on his right forearm. In June 1943, he became a member of the Coast Guard Auxiliary.

The Japanese attack on Pearl Harbor had galvanized Americans in a way not experienced in the past. A sneak attack on their homeland, one not expected by the government or military, set the country's patriotism on fire. That the Japanese took the first step without provocation and caused such complete and enduring damage was unacceptable. Americans were incensed.

Perhaps this explained Lou's determination to join up, coupled with the excitement of the battles and the promised glory depicted in the movies. Perhaps he was also influenced by his brother's enlistment in the Army Air Force, and his brother-in-law Chuck's service in the Navy. It was time to follow in their footsteps.

On November 6, 1943, Lou was drafted into the U.S. Navy as an apprentice seaman, and was sent to boot camp at the Great Lakes Naval Training School in Chicago. He was 30 years old and one of the oldest enlistees in his training class; Irma was 27 and pregnant with their second child.

"I can't believe they are drafting men with children," said Irma's friend Viola, giving her a hug, "and you expecting again." Viola had a young daughter, and the two friends shared parenting tips and celebrated their daughters' achievements.

Congress had passed a law in December 1941 after the Pearl Harbor attack that expanded the draft to include all men between the ages of 18 and 45, even those with children. Viola's husband Orville had been sent to boot camp in Lou's contingent as well; they were assigned to the same barracks—in fact, they were bunkmates.

"I'll only be gone a little while," said Lou. "You'll see I'll be home again before you know it."

"We will miss you so much," said Irma. She mopped up her tears with the hanky she always kept in her sleeve. "It will seem like forever to me. I don't know if I can bear it." She was trying hard to be supportive and to put a good face on this unsettling change in their marriage, but she was scared. Scared for him and for herself, both dealing with the unknown.

November 13

Dear, darling Lou: After you left this morning I did as planned, opened that savings account. Going home wasn't so bad because mom and dad and Lola Lee were there, and Lola kept me amused by opening the stove drawer and throwing everything out. As soon as I would put everything back in she would start all over again. She looked so cute bending over, her little bucket in the air, struggling away. She always made sure everything was out. [After mom and dad and Lola Lee left] I began to feel so lost, everywhere I looked I saw your things. Then Rose [a friend] called and said, "Hello, honey, how are you?" Well, that was all I needed. I started crying and crying. After her call I cried a good bit more and felt much better. Maybe all I needed was a good cry.

—Love, Irma and Lola Lee

November 14

Dear Hubby: Viola called me up and told me you tried to get me on the phone. I was so disappointed because I wasn't home. She told me all you had done and that you expected to go to a movie. What did you see? Also that you boys both wrote us long letters. I hope so. I wonder if I will get them tomorrow? Well, Tuesday anyway. I kept hoping until 10:00 pm tonight that you might call back. But I suppose you couldn't. Do you miss me? I miss you. Vi and I went into town and decided to go to a movie when you tried to call. I have a feeling Viola and I will be fast friends. She's very sweet and sincere. And we have so much in common. I hope you and Orville will be the same.

Today, going to Viola's I saw our little buggy [automobile] standing on the corner. I felt so bad. She looked so out of place in

a row with all the other cars. She looked like she was begging for a garage. I almost went over and talked to her. But I was afraid someone would think I was crazy.

I'll call your mom and dad tomorrow and let them know you are ok.

—Love, Wify and Baby

November 14

Dear Hon: I miss you so, and Lola Lee too. How is everything at home? Monday is the big day for us. If we pass our exams, we are in for good, if not, we'll be sent home. Boy, there are a lot of young kids here. Please, hon, call up the folks and tell them I am ok. I will close now, going to chow soon.

—Loads of love, Lou

November 18

Dear Lou: I saw and rented the apartment [on Central Avenue] today on the third floor. It is $17.75 for the three rooms including heat, gas, and light. The apartment is rather small, but it has a lot of closet space and I'm sure after I get used to it, I'll like it. I'm moving tomorrow, 8:00 a.m. How are you? Everyone got your address cards today. I got a letter from the Navy department telling me you're there safe. Write to my new address.

—Love, Irma

November 21

Dear Lou: Still arranging and rearranging. We really have too much furniture. Can you imagine all our bedroom furniture and the baby's two pieces in a room smaller than the one we had [in the other apartment]? I have the cedar hope chest and sewing machine in the hall. It isn't too crowded. The living room is hard

to fix too. It is larger, but you know with our furniture we need so many corners. Lola Lee walks all over the place. She finally touched the radiator tonight and learned what hot means. We miss you so much and will more so for Thanksgiving. How are things with you? P.S. Write to me.

—Love, Irma

Moving away from the security of the Hungarian neighborhood must have increased Irma's anxiety, but the apartment was affordable and she didn't want to live with her parents. She surely lost contact with friends who shared her background and upbringing. Both their families remained in the Lorain Avenue community. Irma didn't have a car so she was reliant on streetcars, buses, and her parents to get around.

"I lived in the housing projects near downtown," she said. "I didn't feel as safe, but it was a nice apartment, better than the first one and it was affordable. Other servicemen's wives lived there too. There were other renters like Italians that I didn't know much about, but I was fine." The neighborhood was diverse, and Irma shared bus rides to the projects with Negros, a new experience with her limited exposure to the world.

November 21

Dearest One: Honey, I am so glad you got into the apartment, even if it is small. At least you have a better place now than before. Gee, darling, I miss you so. And baby Lola Lee too. Sometimes I think this is all a dream and I will wake up and find myself at home. I am feeling fine. But I get blue when I think of you and Lola Lee so far away.

—Loads of love, Lou

November 22

Dear Lou: Mom was in today [from the farm] to help straighten things out. Everything is set pretty well. I like the apartment more and more each day. I'm sure you will too. I keep thinking how nice it would have been if we could have had something like this when we first got married, it sure would have been fun. It is always so nice and warm here.

—Love, Irma

November 23

Dearest Hubby: Lola Lee and I had so much fun walking through the project and stopping at all the small playgrounds to watch the kiddies play. Lola kept shouting at all the children as is her way. Instead of sitting in the buggy, she walked besides the buggy or helped me push it. She looked so darn cute doddling along and trying to keep up.

I got your letter today and was very glad to hear from you. Can't you please write just a little bit more? Maybe twice a week? Please?

Viola paid me a surprise visit tonight. I was glad. I do get tired of listening to the radio.

I hope the shots [vaccinations] aren't too hard on you. I miss you very much. Hope things end soon so as to have you back again. I don't like being a widow.

—Love, Irma & Lola

Lou also received letters from his older sister Margaret and her teenage daughter Jeanne. Margaret exchanged letters with their brother, Johnny, who was stationed first in England, then in Sicily with the Army Air Force. Irma was still harboring resentment against Margaret for not delivering on her promise of supplying a traditional wedding cake for her reception. In one letter, Margaret acknowledged Irma's hurt feelings.

"She should get over it, there are bigger troubles in these times." But Irma never did.

Jeanne's letters were supportive of her uncle's "sailor life" and expressed curiosity about his experiences at boot camp. Mostly they were a delightful accounting of teen life in 1943 while a war raged overseas.

"I am in study hall and I thought I would write to you," she said. "I went roller skating last night and did I have the fun. I was supposed to go bowling tonight with a boy I work with, but my mother is going away so I have to watch my darling little brother. Don, my boyfriend, is taking me to the show tomorrow night. Thursday we are all going to Grandma's for Thanksgiving. Friday I am going roller skating, and Saturday I will most likely go away with Don, and Sunday I will stay at home to do my lovely homework. How do you like the Navy?"

November 24

Dearest Lou: This is Wednesday. Dad is picking us up after work. We are going out to the country [to her parents' farm] for Thanksgiving (That's a laugh). Nothing much happened today and nothing much will happen later either so I'm writing this letter early so I can mail it when dad comes.

Say, by the way, how is your washing coming along? Like it? Be sure to get in practice and then you can help me wash diapers.

Viola and I are going to a movie Sunday afternoon, if she can get her sister to watch the baby.

I'm going to Gertie's [one of the women in her club] for supper Friday and from there to Friday Night Club. Everyone is trying to be so nice [since you were drafted].

—Love-Irma

November 25

Dearest One: I really don't have much time to write as I would like to, believe me, my love, we have to keep our barracks clean. If some men leave something dirty they get a happy hour. What I mean by that is you stand at attention for one hour looking at a clock. So you are wondering when I will be home. That is pretty hard to say. But I hear we may get our boot leave around January 8. Well, that is all I have to say. I better hurry and get some more turkey.

—Love forever, your hubby

November 28

Dear Lou: The days have been so nice for quite awhile, regular autumn weather. Also, the days are so darn long. There's nothing to do. There just isn't anything to look forward to. January seems so far away. And those few leave days will pass swiftly and then nothing but waiting again. Nuts!

Good night, darling. I'll feel better tomorrow.

—Yours, Irma & Lola

December 2

Dearest Lou: Today is my first washday here, believe me I had plenty of clothes. Honestly, it was so easy to wash here I almost fell over from surprise. In the first place, you have plenty of hot water from the beginning right on through. Then everything is so handy, you're through before you know it. The only catch is that you have to have your clothes out of the dryer by 12:30 p.m. so the next woman can have it. So I'll have to do better next time in order for my clothes to dry or else re-hang them in the basement.

—Love, Irma the washwoman

December 4

Dearest Sweet: Today is Saturday and I did my ironing and didn't even have time to take Lola Lee out for a walk. I get tired just thinking of going down and up these stairs with her. She was so darn crabby today and kept wanting to get out of her playpen and into everything. I really think she is getting a little spoiled. And I'm the guilty one. Did I tell you Lola Lee has two more teeth and two coming. That will be ten all told. Honestly, darling, how do you like the Navy life now. Has it come up to your expectations? Do you think you will like it even if it is a little hard now? I honestly hope you like it. We miss you and want you back with us. Our home isn't a home without the big boss.

—Love, Irma & Lola Lee

December 5

Dearest One: So here are a few lines about what we have to do—Get up at 5:30 a.m. Be outside at 5:40 a.m., then run around 4 or 6 blocks and then we have exercise of all kinds. Then we drill with rifles and march around for four hours. Then we go to school for rope knots and all sorts of knots. Then we drill some more and more. And we have to swim 50 yards once a week. No wonder you can't buy lard or Ivory soap at home or ice cream and candy, it is all here. So if you need any soap, let me know, and I will bring some home when we leave. I took out a $10,000 insurance policy for you, just in case. Let me know as soon as you get the government allowance. Will close to get ready for chow.

—Love from your old man, Lou

December 5

Dearest Sweet Lou: I washed diapers in the morning and kept drying them by the radiator. Lola Lee kept pulling all the wet clothes off the chairs onto the floor all day. I made some curtains for the kitchen this evening while listening to the radio. (What did people do before radios, I wonder? Especially service wives.) We miss you much of late. There just doesn't seem to be any future. Hope you had a nice Sunday. Pleasant dreams, dear, dream of us will you?

—Love, Wife

Irma had grown up with radio and, like most Americans, relied on it heavily for entertainment. She could only afford a little plastic Bakelite radio; many families had large fine wood furniture cabinets they gathered around in the evenings.

"I really loved listening to Bing Crosby and the Tommy Dorsey Orchestra," she said. In her faint reedy voice she would sing along to "I'm in the Mood for Love." One of the popular tunes that played on the radio was "I Wish That I Could Hide Inside This Letter." It expressed Lou's feelings of loneliness so he sent her the words in one of his letters. It certainly expressed their longing for one another. Not surprisingly, romantic songs were Irma's favorite, especially those from the movies.

Irma loved the dramatic "soap operas," originally sponsored by Proctor & Gamble's Ivory soap and other detergent brands. The most popular of these heart-wrenching daytime serials of domestic life were *One Man's Family, Our Gal Sunday,* and *The Romance of Helen Trent*. One of the most popular radio shows in history was the detective story *The Shadow Knows*, introduced in 1930. "Who knows what evil lurks in the hearts of men? The Shadow knows!" was the opening line followed by a blood-curdling laugh and pounding organ music.

When World War II began, the radio was the primary source for updates on military battles across the world as well as challenges faced by the home front populace. From 1933 to 1944, President Franklin D. Roosevelt broadcast his Sunday *Fireside Chats* while some 30 million worried listeners tuned in to hear his soothing message of courage and hope in the face of the Great Depression and the Second World War. Irma and other war wives depended on radio broadcasts to provide updates about the battlefront, especially when it became apparent that military censors would delete battlefront information from servicemen's letters, leaving war wives to guess about their husbands' whereabouts.

The radio also broadcast official messages from the government's Office of Price Administration (OPA) to urge listeners to buy war bonds, plant vegetables in their victory gardens, and learn food preparation tips in the face of rationing.

"They advertise war bonds all the time on the radio," Irma said to her friend Rose. "Lou buys them through his Navy paycheck."

December 7

Dearest Husband: From your letter I gather you won't be home for Xmas. Can't you even make it for a few hours? Just get a leave for Chicago and then fly home and fly back. Please try, I can't imagine how I can spend Xmas without you. About the telephone, I've had one since the Friday I moved in. I thought you knew. All you would have to do is call our old number and they would have referred you to our new one. The number is PR. 5275. I must confess I've been disappointed that you haven't called.

—Love, Love, Love, Love and
Loads of kisses, Irma & Lola Lee

(Date missing)

There is another service wife next door to me. But she's never home so I haven't seen her yet. But I know all about her from the people that come to see her and ask about her at my door. She has a baby too. She comes home late at night and then turns the radio on full. She's deaf and has to, I guess. The other night someone called the police at 1:00 a.m. She must be a hot number. The other night she had people over all night. That was Saturday night. They carried on like they were the only ones here (and our bedroom is next to her living room). They finally left Sunday morning at 6:15 a.m., chattering and laughing all the way down three flights of stairs. After they left I thought, "Ah, now sleep!" But no, she put the radio on again! I thought maybe her husband came home on leave. But I didn't see or hear anyone after that. You may think I'm complaining about her. I'm not. I don't mind. I like noise and to hear people. I don't feel so alone. Anyway, it's something for me to think about and laugh over.

How've you been? Miss me and Lola? We miss you. We always talk about and wonder what you are doing at this or that time. How's the food? Would you like any cookies? Canned fruit? Money?

I wonder what's with my allotment? I suppose that's a longer wait yet. Have you heard anything yet? Did you get paid? Or expect to?

—Love, Irma & Lola

December 8

Dear Lou: My allotment check came today. It is $80.00 and does look good. I promise to be a good girl and spend it only where it has to go. There was a blackout test tonight. I wasn't a bit afraid. To prove it, I stayed in my own apartment instead of going over to the DeRosa's [the Italian family in the project]. That's the name

of the family I wrote you about to one side of me. They are Italian and she cooks just like one, garlic and all. I think I'm going to like her. She has a cute little Butch. I can hardly wait for mine or ours. And he [our Butch] can hardly wait to arrive it seems. Kicks all the time.

—Love, Me & Kiddies

December 8

Dearest Sweet: Well, Dear, I finally have big news for you. Will be home 8 of January if nothing happens. Gee, honey, will I be glad to get home and see all of you and Lola Lee too. I bet Lee is prettier and cuter than ever. I miss you all very much. So much, dear, that I can't put it in writing. So you want to know if I like Navy life or not. Well, dear, at first I did not like it at all. But I've kinda gotten used to it. And sometimes I don't give a damn what happens to me. Now, don't feel bad or sorry for me, you know, I always wanted to be in the Navy. Well, I'm in now, so I have to make the best of it. If you need money, let me know. We got paid today, a whole $5.00, that makes it $7.75 that we got. They took $2.25 out of first $5.00 for a few toilet amenities. Well, so long, sweet, will write soon.

—Love, Lou

December 9

Dearest Lou: I washed again today and just can't get used to being done so fast and so easily. To think I used to slave all day in the basement on washday [at the old apartment]. It's wonderful.

I keep reading your last letter over and over. And it keeps me pepped up so. You are just wonderful, honey. Me loves you.

Mother took Lola out to the farm tonight, so I am beginning to feel lonely and lost already. The little rascal sure can fill a day up, nights too for that matter.

Nothing more to report today, so I think I'll close. Goodnight, dear, please dream of me and I'll dream of you. Bargain?
—Love-Irma, Lola Lee, Butch

In the early 1940s, the United States was slowly pulling out of the Great Depression. Once war was declared, the country had to change course and ramp up its manufacturing of war materials. Soon the country was facing food and gasoline shortages and rising prices. The military provided a growing and dependable source of jobs and pay, so hundreds of young men marched off to war, providing their families with steady, if inadequate, income.

According to the U.S. Bureau of Labor Statistics (BLS), food prices increased as much as 50 per cent between 1939 and 1945, depending on the area of the country. In Cleveland, prices increased 42 per cent between 1943 and 1945, making them the highest in the region.

To control rising prices, the government instituted price controls in 1943 for most food staples tracked by the BLS. Because of large government purchases for the military and the difficulty of obtaining foods produced by countries now involved in the war, shortages occurred for some foods, like sugar, on the home front.

A civilian food-rationing program was instituted to ensure that those at all socioeconomic levels would share equally in obtaining foods in short supply. In reality, a black market developed almost immediately for those who knew how to access it. Sugar was rationed according to family size beginning in 1943. One stamp from the War Ration Book One equaled one pound of sugar, and families could redeem one stamp per family member weekly.

According to a Gallup Poll conducted at the end of the war, sugar was the rationed item housewives had missed the most. Butter was the second most coveted food staple, because margarine was not in wide use in the early 40s, and various cooking oils disappeared. As margarine became more common, housewives squeezed dabs of yellow food color into the white margarine so it would resemble butter.

A point system for rationing meats, butter, fat and oils, and cheese required red stamps supplied in War Ration Book Two. Blue stamp rationing covered canned, bottled, and frozen foods. Ration stamps became a kind of currency that required planning to "spend" points allocated to each person within the time stipulated.

In January 1943, Irma's brother Chuck wrote home from his naval base in New York. "I know that they're rationing more and more, but it can't last forever, so you have something to look forward to. We're all alive too, so I guess we're pretty lucky at that. It's a war and I think we're all feeling it now."

In the face of these rationing requirements, women who lived on farms or small towns had the benefit of planting Victory Gardens and canning the harvest for later consumption. Women who lived in cities were told to think of new ways to prepare old favorites. Food industry companies advertised new dishes, and some women's magazines suggested new recipes and doing "more with less."

Newly published cookbooks helped housewives work with what was available. *Good Housekeeping* magazine published a cookbook in 1943 that featured a special section with recipes using rationed foods. Articles were published monthly in the magazine providing shopping and cooking hints using ration coupons. An article titled "If Butter is Scarce" in the March 1944 issue presented helpful hints to stretch allotted butter rations by preparing butter spreads using jams, peanut butter or honey.

December 10

Dear Lou: I wrote out Xmas cards today. Went shopping also. But it's so hard to get anything. It was such a nice day everyone and their grandmother were in town. It took me fully 45 minutes

to cash in my allotment check at May's [department store]. The line was a block long.

Got your letter today. I'm awfully sorry you feel like you do about everything. I'm sure later when things get easier you'll like it. It's just that it's new now and everything is so much harder.

Went out with the girls tonight. We celebrated Gertie's birthday. We went to the New China to eat and to the Allen [movie theater]. I came home by myself after, aren't I brave?

After you get out of training, everything will be better, you'll see. After you start getting short leaves and you can go places, you won't be so sick of it. Just keep thinking of all the nice things we'll do when you get home and time will pass faster.

I'm just dying for you to see our place. And have you sit in your favorite green easy chair. Good night, dear.

—Lots of Love, Irma and Lola

December 11

Dearest Sweet Lou: Was in town all day, shopping for your gifts. I tried very hard to get you a good fountain pen set. But after spending yesterday and part of today looking for a set, I must admit I'm finished. They have cheap-made pens for good money, but we have that kind of pen here [at home]. So I bought you some other things. I hope you'll like them. Please don't open the box until Xmas, dear, otherwise there won't be anything for you to look at on Xmas Eve.

Another thing, if you should find you don't need something amongst those few pieces after opening the box, just don't use it and when you come home we can exchange it for something else.

After shopping until the stores closed tonight, I went to a movie in town, bundles and all.

Don't worry, I'm not buying a lot of things. But it just takes so long to get any one thing that it seems you can buy only two or three pieces a whole day.

Wish you were home with us, darling. This is going to be a hell of a Xmas without you. I thought I would have an artificial tree and keep it up after Xmas until you get home. You may not think that is a good idea. Let me know, will you?

—Love, Irma

December 12,

Dearest Sweet One: Since last Thursday, dear, I have been so busy because our company [in boot camp] is working in the mess hall. I am in charge of six men to wash dishes and plates and what not. Gee, honey, I would sooner wash dishes with you and same with the clothes. It sure is hell washing your own clothes with hand and brush. Every company gets one week of mess work, it is called service work. And then next week we go on workweek. We stand guard on board ship, it will be damn cold out there. Will be on for two hours and off for two hours. It is cold enough to freeze water now. You know this will be the first Xmas that we will not be together. So will call you up Xmas night and say sweet nothings to you, honey. You should see how the food is wasted, what is left over is thrown out and good food, too. Well, this is all I can write at the moment, the boys are coming in for their chow. Here is ten dollars for phone calls, hon.

—So long, honey baby, until next time, Lou

December 13

Dearest Darling: When I called you last night, it was wonderful to hear you talk, it picked me right up. Your voice sounded so pretty to me. For a while, I could not fall asleep, kept thinking about you, dear, and Lola Lee too. Well, when I got up this morning, it was one degree below outside. It was plenty cold in our barracks. We have those hot water heaters, but it does not heat good when the boys wash their clothes, they use up the hot water, so that's it. Wish you would sleep with me now, so you could cover me up when I kick the blanket off. Orville is a lucky guy because when I wake up at night most of my blankets are on top of him. I guess I didn't tell you before we sleep [in neighboring bunks].

How are both my mother and dad? Gee, when a person is away from home that's when they miss everybody, especially his little woman.

—I love you, dear sweet wife, Lou

December 14

Dearest Sweet Irma: Well, another company went on their boot leave, lucky stiffs. It kind of got me down and blue too to see them go and me here yet. But I said to myself, listen kid, you have only three more weeks to go.

Isn't that wonderful, hon, only 21 more days and I will be home. Don't forget to try and get dad's car for us and will try to see everybody. I would really like that, wouldn't you? But would you care to hear our Navy song:

Here comes the Navy, fighting and sea-going crew.
Make way for the Navy, Navy with anchors away.
Everybody loves the Navy of the U.S.A.A.A.

Well there it is, hon, pretty good, no?

—Love, Lou

December 14

Dearest Old Man of Mine: I had a feeling you couldn't make it for Xmas and yet I kept hoping. But the next best thing will be hearing your voice. Mom and Dad will be in for Xmas day because I have the tree. It won't be too bad, we'll keep thinking of each other. O.K.? Anyway, you'll be home soon after that. Besides, with

such a sweet little daughter, I do have a lot to be thankful for. We can hope that by next Xmas holidays we all of us will be together.

—Love, Irma

December 15

Dearest One: You know, dear, I am getting good at sewing socks, and buttons on my pea coat. Just got through with my coat, and then have some more washing to do. How are [the folks], I really miss them all, so may dear God take care of all of them for me. And how are you, dearest, do you think of me now and then like you say. You're always on my mind, dear. Oh boy, I can hardly wait until that boot leave comes around and I'll see all of my dear ones that I miss so, especially you, dearest darling, my brave little mate.

—Yours forever, Lou

December 15

How are you? I sure hope you don't develop a cold. You are always so sick with one. Yes, it is too bad I can't be there close to you so as to tuck you in at least once in awhile.

I suppose you boys will be so tired when you do come home you'll need all the time to recuperate. So I'm not making too many plans for running around. Maybe you can rest during the day and we can spend the nights visiting and having friends in (if I can get them to come here).

I got a letter from you yesterday and today. I couldn't believe my eyes. You are very sweet, dear. Did I ever tell you? I love you very, very much.

—Love from all of us

December 18

Dearest Lou of Mine: I'm finishing some blouses for Lola Lee's skirts. She is going to have three skirts and blouses. They didn't cost me much. I'm sure if we were to buy them for her it would have run all of $15.00 and that's no lie. I can hardly wait to put them on her, but we must wait until Santa Claus brings them to her. I feel so guilty because she's not getting as much as other kids are getting that we know. But I just can't put out any more money for her. Besides, she'll have the [doll] buggy. She'd rather have her dad here than anything else anyway.

Love—Family

December 20

Darling Dearest: All day long I waited for tonight. The later it got the more nervous I got thinking maybe you couldn't get through. The thought of hearing your voice in the evening made me so peppy all day. I just worked and worked, thinking the harder I worked the faster the time will pass, and soon evening will come. And it seemed evening would never, never come. Then about 8:00 some girl called and said she was calling about a radio poll. Asked me all kinds of questions about what programs I listened to and who the sponsors were. I was so nervous all the while for fear you would want to get through about that time. I gave her some very crazy answers. I'm afraid she didn't have a very good opinion of me when she finally hung up. Oh well!

Now that I've talked to you, I don't feel like working anymore. I just want to sit and daydream about you, about us, and everything. I want to close my eyes and remember every word you said and feel sorry with you about the bad things and feel good with you about the good things.

It makes me feel so very close to you for a little while. I love you, darling, more than ever and wish we could be close together again as we were before.

—Love, Irma

Once the war started the shortage of suitable fabrics for clothing was challenging, especially when textile rationing began. Ready-to-wear clothes had gained acceptance but were costly to purchase. Like other women, Irma reused—*make do or reuse* was the slogan—dress fabrics for her own clothes and for the children's. She made her daughter's playclothes and dresses, decorating them with flowers and leaves embroidered on the collars or bodice. Irma also embroidered tablecloths, dishtowels, pillowcases, and other household linens as her mother had.

December 31

Dear Lou: I want you to have one perfect time when you get home [from boot camp]. I do hope you shall be happy. How can I ever get through this week?

Again, about getting to the apartments. You take the Central bus at E. 2nd and Prospect. (The street is back of May Co. exactly opposite May Co.'s back). Get off at 24th & Central, cross Central. Go through the project arch, take the first walk to your right, walk three flights up and rap at #329. And wait for us to fly into your arms.

Write us what time to expect you. Come by train, it's much faster. Write anything else I need to know. I think I've written everything to you. Except I Love Love, Love you. Please, please hurry, hurry home.

—Irma

Happy times with Lou on one of his leaves. (1943)

Chapter 4

1944: Daddy All Gone

Jan. 25, 1944, 1.
Tues day.

Dear Beloved Husband:
Just another day closer to seeing you again. For, from now on each day I'm going to try and push fast so the next one will come and with it sweet lovable you.
I cleaned house today, did some sewing and tended our daughter. We have our little fights together, she wants her way

Lou returned home on leave in January when Navy boot camp was finally over. Irma and Lola Lee and the rest of Irma's family were waiting for him at the apartment. Irma kept watching for him from the balcony. When she saw him coming up the street looking very jaunty in his sailor hat with his seabag slung over his shoulder, she shouted, "Lou! Lou!" and ran down the stairs.

Lou put down his bag and grabbed her in a big hug.

"I'm so glad to be home with my girls," he said. He gave her a loving kiss, as romantic as any she had seen at the movies.

"Oh," he said, backing away from her large belly, "I see the new baby is almost here!"

Irma's parents and her brother Chuck, also home on leave, came down the stairs. Her mother was holding Lola Lee, who was studying her father's face. They all spilled out on the sidewalk, talking happily and hugging and kissing each other.

"Lola Lee," said Irma, "give your daddy a kiss." The little hand reached out to her father. He took her in his arms and gave her soft cheek a kiss.

"I'm so happy to see my little darling again," he said.

Lou was glad to be finished with boot camp, and some of his experiences there had given him second thoughts about his enlistment. He shared his disappointments with Irma, who discussed them with Chuck.

"I don't want to be one of those 'I told you so fellows,'" Chuck said, "but when you wrote about Lou's shattered illusions of the great Navy I can't help but think of the many times I'd warned him of the non-glamorous Navy life. He'll kick himself for even thinking he wanted to join up. Well, like they say, experience is the best teacher. He'll eventually accustom himself to the hand fate gave him in the Navy."

The couple spent time with family and friends, visiting their old haunts, until Lou's leave ended two weeks later. They said their goodbyes at the train station, clinging to each other tightly, fearful of what was to come. They didn't know what was in store for Lou in his first deployment in the war, and Irma worried that he wouldn't return in time for the birth of their child.

A goodbye dinner before Lou joins his crew on the USS Bull. (1944)

January 23

Dearest Lou: When you left at the station last week Sunday, I had a little idea in the back of my mind that you'd probably be stationed somewhere close enough to come home over weekends. It really never entered my mind that it would be the last time I would see you for a long time. Please say it's not so. I just can't bear to think of you so far away and maybe going further.

The coming of Butch [the new baby] is so close now. It will keep me busy fixing the clothes, so will have little time for tears. Lola Lee kept looking for you in the bed in the morning. Then would say, "Daddy all gone" and I would show her your picture and she would say "Love Daddy." And honestly, hon, she hugs the picture and kisses your face.

Will write more tomorrow, dear hubby of mine. I hope I get a letter from you soon. Meantime we all send our love and kisses, oodles and oodles of them.

—Irma & Lola Lee

January 29

Dearest Lou: Haven't much to say tonight. Have had the blues all night. Miss you so much, dear. When will it all end?

I keep worrying about our baby coming early again. I haven't even a name. Will you please send me some names you'd like?

Aren't you ever going to write me again?

Loads of love to you, dear sweet husband of mine.

—Your "Crabby" Wife Irma & Lola Lee

February 5

Dear Love: Was home all day today. Waited for your call, but didn't do much of anything. Slept-ate-and-listened to the radio.

Please give me a nice quiet straitjacket to crawl in, this whole big world is crazy. Listening to these radio commentators, senators, congressmen, big business men, and men who should know, I have now come to the conclusion we're all crazy and don't know it.

I am thankful I'm not a man and therefore don't get in trouble. But believe me if I were, I wouldn't move a finger towards a gun or a toe towards marching until I'd find out what it is all about. And I'm afraid I'd rot in jail, because there is no answer.

—Your Loving Wify, Irma

Irma was a pacifist all her life. Americans in general came to accept the war as unavoidable after Pearl Harbor was bombed in 1941, but over time she came to consider the war a futile effort.

Unlike other families around her with breadwinners in the home, Irma had to run the household on her monthly family allotment check from the government. As the United States shifted into wartime mode and more soldiers and sailors with families were drafted, Congress increased family allotments for wives and children. The Servicemen's Dependents Allowance Act of 1942 was passed to help servicemen meet their family's economic needs on the home front, with allowances for dependents throughout the war and for six months afterward.

The wife of a serviceman with two children received a monthly allotment from the government of $100. If more children were born during the war, the military would pay $100 in maternity benefits, including prenatal and pediatric care, and increase the allotment. In addition, servicemen could purchase a $10,000 life insurance policy at a reasonable cost.

Starting pay for servicemen of all branches of the armed forces was set in 1943 at $50.00 a month. For each dependent, pay was increased $20.00. Overseas duty provided a 20 percent boost in pay or $10 a month for enlisted men based on their rank. Married servicemen were expected to contribute $22 of their pay each month to their wife as part of the Family Allotment Program. Servicemen pay was purportedly set to match the average civilian worker's wages, but the amount was not adequate to support a family's needs.

As inflation continued to rise, housewives were challenged to stretch their allotment check to cover living costs. Because Irma was a child of immigrants and the Great Depression, her expectations of life were molded by growing up during hard times when everyone made the most of what little they had. As the war wore on, Irma became quite anxious over making ends meet. She and her friend Viola, whose husband was also serving on a Navy ship, were in similar situations and shared their fears.

"I can barely pay my bills," Irma said. "How will we ever catch up with other families after the war?" She and other war wives, struggling to live on military pay, were hard-pressed to save money for an uncertain future when the family was reunited.

When Lou completed a Navy training course for seaman first class, he earned a small pay hike that he shared with Irma. He also sent additional money home to help Irma with expenses from time to time.

"After all," he said, "I don't have anywhere to spend my pay out here."

February 9

Darling Lou of Mine: I just can't and won't believe they are taking you away from me.

It is bad enough for you to be away from our family circle [and stationed in New York City], let alone out of the country so soon.

All tonight I have been seeing you on a dark and dreary boat slowly leaving a dark harbor in New York. The whole picture is so dismal and forlorn, I just can't bear it.

This all came so sudden. I expected you to be around for months yet. You can't have learned everything [about the ship] in so short a time.

But, darling, you have my complete love. That will help you come through. And then there is your sweet daughter. And soon, your Butch. Surely, all these things will help keep you going at hard moments.

Goodnight, darling, sweetheart, lover, husband of mine, Lou, dear.

—Love, Irma

Lou received orders to proceed to the East Coast to join the crew of the USS *Bull*, a high-speed destroyer transport (APD) developed for use in World War II. About the length of a football field at 306 feet, the widest part or beam of the ship was 37 feet; it housed 162 sailors. The *Bull* could only travel at 24 knots (20.9 mph). Although it lacked the speed and firepower of destroyers, it had the capability of dropping depth charges and the maneuverability required for a submarine hunter.

Commissioned as a transatlantic Navy convoy escort for the European theatre, the *Bull* transported military supplies to Ireland for use by the troops. On his first voyage to Ireland in February, Lou experienced forceful North Atlantic winds as the ship sailed through a powerful hurricane. The ship was scheduled to support naval operations on Normandy's beaches on June 6, but it received orders to return to the shipyards in New York City. The *Bull's* last European voyage as a destroyer escort for supply convoys ended in July 1944.

February 9

*Dearest One: Well, here I am in my new home, dear. It sure feels funny to be on it [*the *USS Bull]. But she is a honey; you should see it, shiny and powerful. Oh, darling, I would give anything to be home with you instead of being here. But will have to make the best of it as long as I am here. The fellows all seem to be swell, they all try to help us with everything. Going up to Portland, Maine, for gunner practice. I know you won't like this, sweet, me going so far away. But there isn't anything we can do about it but pray to God that our ship brings us back safely. I know, dearest, that I will come back to you and the kids for our lives will be spent together. It can't end any other way.*

The only thing I feel bad about is I won't see our little Butch...

Well, dearest, sweet wife of mine, this is all I can say at this time, the boys are hitting the bunk, so I will too.

—Love and more love, from your sailor boy, Lou

USS Bull in port. (1945)

February 12

Dearest Lou: It was so wonderful to hear your voice [when you returned to port]. It just peps me up so.

But when I got your letter this morning, it was swell too. A letter I can read over and over again. I can remember most of it too. But I'm never sure that I have remembered all of it.

Besides I never say everything I mean to say [on the phone] and I get so mad at myself. Is it that way with you too?

—Love to my hubby

February 15

Dearest Husband of Mine: I meant to write so many times, dear, I'm so glad you like your ship. Also that you found a buddy. I was sorry to hear that you are broke. That I don't like. Did you get paid as you expected today? I always meant to ask you how much you get and how much a month, would like to get straightened out on the subject.

I ordered my glasses today, shell rims and all for only $12.00. Doctor only charged $3.00 instead of usual $5.00 for examina-

tion when I told him you were in the Navy. The last time I had completely new glasses, it cost me more than $20.00.

I also bought myself a corduroy robe for the hospital. It is a pretty shade of blue and I got red slippers. I wanted to make the ones I had at home do, but the robes were too small and the slippers were shabby.

I also bought a pair of blue bunny slippers for Lola Lee. Hon, you should see how pleased she was with them. She kept looking down at them all evening. She'd forget them for a few minutes and then remember and look down and give the cutest pleased smile.

—Love, love to you

February 20

Dearest Mine: Another day and no phone call. Well, maybe tomorrow. I hope everything is well with you.

I've been trying to decide on some names for our baby. It is pretty hard without you here. Here are some, will you tell me which ones you like. The ones I like best are on the top.

Boys:

Blair—my favorite

Allen, Wayne, Roger, Raymond, Ramon, Lowell, Glen, Edwin, Conrad, Craig, Barry

Combine them or add another that sounds good to the names. I want the children to have a middle name, don't you, dear?

Girls:

Diana—my favorite

Vivian

Well, go to it, dear. Take a pick. I'll see if you pick what I like. You know just everyone says I'm going to have a boy. Happy, huh!

—Love—Irma & children

February 21

Dear Lou: Went to the doctor today. Everything seems fine. I inquired about that maternity aid. I really should have applied when you first told me. But I still may get some of it [the maternity aid] if the baby doesn't come for two weeks. It takes that long for it to go through the [federal government's] Columbus, Ohio, office.

I went right down to get an application and filled it out and sent it in this evening's special delivery to the doctor...she promised to send it special delivery to Columbus after filling it out.

How are you, dear? Don't worry about us. We have been feeling fine, except I wish I could know where you are.

—Love, Irma

Censorship of mail was intended to prevent exposure of U.S. troop positions in the various theaters of war to the enemy. "Loose Lips Sink Ships" was the Navy's motto. Lou's mail was routed through the San Francisco Fleet Post Office. Beginning in 1944 and continuing until the Japanese surrendered in 1945, each piece of mail had to be read, initialed, and stamped "passed" by naval censors. If the censors felt that a section of a letter was too revealing, they confiscated the letter. A soldier might never know that a letter did not reach his loved one. A few of Lou's letters showed censors at work—information apparently deemed sensitive had been snipped out.

Lou's niece Jeanne, in high school at the time, wrote him sporadically, and in one of her letters she wrote "HI! MR. CENSORER! IS THIS LETTER OK?" at the top of the letter. It must have been because the letter was delivered. She mainly discussed her dating life and boyfriends, so the censors probably weren't too worried.

Lou was careful to avoid mentioning the *Bull's* exact locations, so Irma, like other war wives, had the worrisome task of trying to figure out exactly where he was by listening to the radio, watching movie newsreels, and reading newspapers. Although newspapers and broadcasts described the ferocious battles underway in the Pacific, the movie newsreels captured the battles too realistically. It was, however, difficult for Irma to pinpoint when and where the *Bull* was involved.

"I'm always afraid to watch the newsreels," she said. "What if I see the *Bull* in one of the terrible battles? I couldn't bear it."

February 24

Dearest Hubby: Oh dear, do you know how good it is to hear from you? I imagined everything waiting to hear from you. And when you called and the operator connected us, I was sure you were in town and my dreams came true, but no such luck!

Although Boston is a long way off, at least I know you are in the states and that should be enough for me. I just won't believe you'll be going out after this, dear, on active duty. I keep hoping I will be pleasantly surprised like the last time.

Write me, dear, and phone me when you can. Miss you awfully. Wish this darn war would end already. I'm so very much fed up with it. Good night, dear. I'll dream of you, such sweet dreams.

—Yours, Irma

February 29

Dear Daddy: I hope you are not too disappointed that our son is a girl. If you are now, you'll get over it when you see her.

She really is the exact opposite of Lola Lee. Our new baby has such dark brown hair, almost black, and long. One thing I know will please you is that her ears are real close to her head. I think she'll be a much easier baby to care for than Lola Lee too.

What do you think of her name? Diane-Vivian?

I woke up about 3:15 a.m. on Sunday morning. Mr. DeRosa [our neighbor in the project] took me to the [Fairview Park] hospital [on Lorain Avenue] and I was up in the labor room by 5:40

a.m. I had to be in the labor room all day. They had no rooms until 4:30 in the afternoon. I'm in a ward with four beds.

Chuck telegrammed you Sunday night. The DeRosa's telegrammed you through the Red Cross the next day.

I do hope you can come home [to see your new baby]. There is a girl here who has a Navy husband too. He got home for three days [on leave].

—Irma

Irma carefully chose a middle name for her second born, not a Hungarian custom in the old country. Her hospital room was filled with flowers: daffodils from Lola, roses from Chuck, gladioli from her mother, and carnations from her friend Viola. She missed not being able to share this happy event with Lou. When the husbands of the other home front wives in the hospital visited, it increased her loneliness.

The letters express Irma's disappointment at not having a baby boy. They had hoped for a boy, a "Butch," and she had taken on the responsibility of delivering one for Lou. Old wives tales and much guessing among family and friends increased the disappointment when the predictions proved wrong.

She apparently felt she had to launch a small marketing campaign for her new daughter, starting with pointing out that the baby's ears were flat against her head. Lou was embarrassed that his ears stuck out, and he endured some teasing about his ears "flapping in the wind" from Irma's brother, always a big kidder. He worried that his children would inherit this "flaw." When he finally was home on leave in April to see the new baby he picked her up, and gave a big smile.

"Her ears are so tiny and flat. I'm so happy to see that, Irm," he said, giving the baby a big sloppy kiss.

March 6

Dear Hubby: I was supposed to go home tonight, but decided to wait until tomorrow, the ninth day.

It will be so different from the last time, dear. I won't have you waiting for me. Of course, there will be my folks and Chuck and Lola Lee. But somehow no matter how much they love me it just can't be the same as if you were there to greet me with Lola Lee.

It would be so much fun to introduce our daughters to each other together. I know it will be quite an experience. But I'll write you all about it tomorrow if I'm not too tired after everything settles down.

I never give up hoping you are still in the states and can see your daughter soon.

—Love from your big family—Irma-Lola Lee-Diane

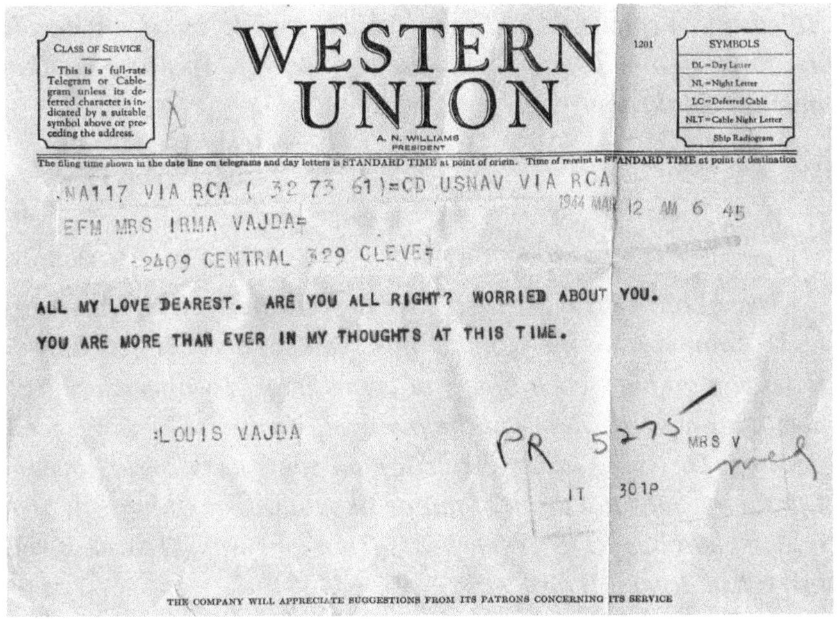

CLASS OF SERVICE
This is a full-rate Telegram or Cablegram unless its deferred character is indicated by a suitable symbol above or preceding the address.

WESTERN UNION
A. N. WILLIAMS PRESIDENT

1201

SYMBOLS
DL=Day Letter
NL=Night Letter
LC=Deferred Cable
NLT=Cable Night Letter
Ship Radiogram

The filing time shown in the date line on telegrams and day letters is STANDARD TIME at point of origin. Time of receipt is STANDARD TIME at point of destination

.NA117 VIA RCA (32 73 61)=CD USNAV VIA RCA
1944 MAR 12 AM 6 45
EFM MRS IRMA VAJDA=
-2409 CENTRAL 329 CLEVE=

ALL MY LOVE DEAREST. ARE YOU ALL RIGHT? WORRIED ABOUT YOU.
YOU ARE MORE THAN EVER IN MY THOUGHTS AT THIS TIME.

:LOUIS VAJDA

PR 5275 MRS V
IT 301P

THE COMPANY WILL APPRECIATE SUGGESTIONS FROM ITS PATRONS CONCERNING ITS SERVICE

March 13

Dearest One, Lou: I received your cablegram about 1400 Navy time, yes—today. To say I was and am stunned [that you are not coming home on leave] is putting it mildly. Things like this just can't happen to you and me. It all seems like a bad dream and I keep hoping to wake up soon and find things all right again in our little family.

Do you like the name I gave her?

Just can't find anything to write about. What does one write to a husband overseas. I must be a patriotic wife and try to keep my spirits up.

I suppose by the time this letter reaches you, you will know about our new family member. Did you get the telegrams or did you learn things through my letters?

I hope you are writing to me regularly now, dear. It was bad enough not getting any mail from you when you were in the states. At least then you could call every once in awhile, but if you decide not to write now you will hurt me very deeply. You owe me that much, I think, don't you?

—Love-Irma-Lola-Diane

April 10

Dear Lou: This is my first letter to you since you left [after his leave home to visit the baby]. I miss you so, dear. It gets harder to let you go back each time you come home. I wonder how you are. What you are doing at the moment, if you are in danger. Or fighting. Or trying to save your life on some dark raging ocean. But then I must not think of things like that. Everything will turn out all right, won't it? A few years from now we will think it was just a bad dream. Won't we?

—Love-Irma-Lola Lee-Diane

April 18

Dear Lou: My friend Ann was over Saturday...She brought Lola three pairs of socks for Easter and brought Diane a blanket for a gift. Her husband is mad because he can't be in the actual battle when he is shipped overseas. I told her you would trade places with him any day. And he wouldn't be so anxious to go out again if he had one dose of it. But I guess people do not know how well off they are. Here they are scrapping and fighting about some little thing or other instead of enjoying each other's company and having a good time while they can. I'm losing patience with this world!

I forgot to mention that the girls in the Friday Club collected $11.00 and gave it to me for the baby. Wasn't that nice of them?

Good night, darling, dream of your family.

—Love-Irma-Lola Lee-Diane

May 28

Dearest One: Well, here I am again, dear. Hope you're not getting tired of reading my letters, "Ha! Ha!" As if there is so many of them. But, darling, sometimes I just don't feel like writing, maybe I am lazy or something. Other times I haven't had much time if you get what I mean. But here I am at the Red Cross Canteen writing to my loved one. Sweet, I love you more than life itself. How many times I wished that you could be here with me. But you would not like it here at all, just like me. There isn't anything interesting to do, but go to a movie and then find out I saw it when I was still at home. Home, gee, that word sounds beautiful, just like you. Think you can make it again? I mean for you to come to New York. I will try to get a leave when we get back. I hope. Hope! Hope! Will close now with loads of love. Me loves you. And loves you

—Love forever, Lou

June 14

Dear Lou: I have just received several of your letters. It is so very nice to hear from you. However, I had quite a letdown because I expected to see you, not hear from you, by this time.

This is my first letter in over a month because I figured you didn't get them anyway.

And that I would see you. So now I guess you are receiving mail there and none comes from me.

We are all fine. The children are growing by leaps and bounds. They are so cute, I just can't believe that they are my or our kids. We all miss you, wish to see you. We all are sending all our love to you, to hold you fast.

—Irma—Lola Lee—Diane

June 18

Dearest Lou: Last night being Saturday, I went to see a movie [while the kids were at the folks']. I saw "Uncertain Glory" with Errol Flynn. I can't say whether I like it or not. I can't stand that Flynn since all the scandal about him.

However, they did have some invasion pictures on the newsreel that I wanted to see. I kept looking for the Bull and yet hoping I'd never see it. I hope you were elsewhere when all this was going on

—Love, Irma

June 20

Dearest Beloved: I received all your letters and the candy too from the children today. It sure makes me feel a lot better when I hear from you. Oh, darling, I miss you all so very much. At times when I think about you and the kids so far away, I could just cry and cry. Sometimes I just can't keep back the tears. I guess I am getting old or something. Oh, well, it won't be long before I can come home on my leave. So you want to know how our trip [to Ireland] was. It was very nice, no action at all. But once we got a sub contact at night. That was one time I was scared stiff. It was so dark, you couldn't see a thing, but we lost them, I guess, or it might have been fish. That was the night I was writing to you and I put that in my letter, so it was censored.

Well, this is goodnight, dear, will write more tomorrow. Always thinking of all of you. I love you, darling.

—Lou

JUNE 21

DEAREST ONE: I WISH YOU COULD BE HERE WITH ME LIKE WE WERE IN NEW YORK [FOR OUR HONEYMOON]. I MISS YOU MORE THAN EVER. I WISH THAT I COULD CALL YOU EVERY OTHER NIGHT. I WILL CALL YOU ON SUNDAY NIGHTS AS WE PLANNED. AFTER THAT I WILL NOT CALL YOU AS MUCH AS I DID BEFORE.

I HAVE TO CLOSE NOW BECAUSE THE USO BUDDIES CLUB IS ABOUT TO CLOSE...GOODNIGHT MY LOVE...WILL SAY AGAIN THAT I LOVE YOU MORE THAN LIFE ITSELF...

—YOUR DEAREST HUSBAND, LOU

June 27

Dear Lou: It seems strange that out of our crowd only you are gone [to war]. Here everyone is buying houses or other things and we are more in the hole than ever. They do all the complaining and I'm supposed to keep my mouth shut, after all I get $100.00 a month, what more do I want?

Hope you are in better spirits. We all miss you.

—Love-Irma-Lola Lee-Diane

P.S. I'm sending you a few dollars to spend.

In July, Lou's ship returned to its base in New York City to prepare for a new role in the war. Over the next three months, the *Bull* underwent conversion to a high-speed troop transport at Todd's Shipyards in Brooklyn. The crew received training to support the new mission: transporting and supporting the needs of the Underwater Demolition Troops (UDTs) Special Forces. Lou gained a new job as a gunner on one of the antiaircraft guns.

The UDTs, also known as "frogmen," were a new combat "weapon" for use in the Pacific War. The *Bull* could transport about 100 UDTs and their gear—fins, swim shoes, knives, and face masks—shuttling them to their assignments on one Japanese island or another for the duration of the war. UDTs played a crucial role in the amphibious operations to secure the islands in the Pacific on the path toward invading Japan.

Once the *Bull's* conversion was underway, Lou was able to go home on leave in August for twenty-one days. During September and October, while the *Bull* was still in dry dock in New York City, Irma made several trips from Cleveland to be with Lou. Her mother's sister Agnes gave them the use of her apartment while she visited with Lila in Cleveland. Lou and Irm saw all the new movies and went to Coney Island where they posed for photos behind a cutout of a cardboard boat, Irma looking uncomfortable, and Lou smiling broadly. They bought matching silhouettes of themselves made of black cutout paper. Lou's sailor cap and Irma's perky hat were captured in profile.

"Silhouettes were quite popular," Irma said. "They were a nice remembrance of New York." When she returned home she framed them and hung them in the hallway of the apartment. When the children were older, Irma added silhouettes of them to the family photo wall as well.

They collected fond memories of all the sights they shared in New York during their visits, and these would be a comfort in the months ahead. Compared to other servicemen and their wives, Lou and Irm had spent a significant amount of time together in 1944.

Fun times in NYC while Lou is off duty. (1944)

August 22

Darling: You've been gone one day and already it seems like a week. We miss you. Lola Lee got up this morning and kept chattering and pointing to the bed and saying "bye-bye." I think she knows you are gone for a while again.

I hope you stay in New York for a long time (as long as the war lasts). If you do have to go before the war ends, I hope I can go to New York and see you.

Mrs. DeRosa was around to ask the Friday Club girls for a spaghetti dinner Thursday, so things have a way of going on.

We all miss you much, dad. We think you are the most wonderful and best dad a family ever had.

Love from your three girls—Irma-Lola Lee-Diane

P.S. Just got your call, dear. I was so lonesome for your voice. But, really, I shouldn't complain. I had you [home] longer than I expected and I have seen you more than most war wives see their husbands.

—Love-Love-Love from all of us to you.

XXXXXXXXXXX

OOOO

SEPTEMBER 4

DEAREST IRMA: WELL HERE I AM TYPING ANOTHER LETTER TO YOU, SWEET. WILL TRY TO MAKE THIS ONE LONGER. AS YOU KNOW BY NOW, AM BACK ON MY POST STARTING THIS MORNING AT EIGHT. WILL BE THROUGH AT FOUR, THEN WILL CLEAN UP AND SEE A SHOW.

SPEAKING ABOUT SHOWS, HAVE JUST ABOUT SEEN ALL OF THEM. BUT HAVE SAVED THE BEST OF THEM FOR LAST SO THAT WE CAN SEE THEM TOGETHER WHEN YOU COME DOWN TO ME. TODAY IS THE DAY I CALL YOU UP. IT SURE WILL BE SWELL TO HEAR YOUR VOICE AGAIN, DARLING.

BUT YOU BETTER HURRY. THIS TIME I HEARD THAT WE SHOVE OFF MIDDLE OF OCTOBER INSTEAD OF DECEMBER. SO TRY AND MAKE IT SOON AS YOU CAN, OK? HOW IS EVERYONE AT HOME? THOSE TWO LITTLE STINKERS, ARE THEY ALL RIGHT? I BET YOU HAVE YOUR HANDS FULL, MAYBE THAT'S WHY I DIDN'T HEAR FROM YOU.

I DON'T KNOW WHAT IS WRONG WITH ME. I CAN'T THINK OF ANYTHING TO SAY. AND WHEN I DO, I CAN'T SPELL OUT THE WORDS. SO FROM NOW ON WILL LOOK IT UP IN THE BOOK.

I HAVE A WATCH TUESDAY AT MIDNIGHT TO EIGHT IN THE MORNING. THEN I AM FREE UNTIL THURSDAY. SO YOU CAN SEE, DEAR, WHEN YOU GET HERE, WE WILL BE TOGETHER EVERY DAY.

—LOU

When she went to New York in October to be with Lou, Irma worked in a retail store while he was on duty. These trips to New York were a strain on their budget.

"I have to tell you I'm broke to come to New York right now," she wrote in one of her letters, "but I would never forgive myself if I didn't have these last few weeks with you."

On October 5 they attended a ship's dance for the *Bull's* crew at the Roosevelt Hotel on Madison Avenue and 45th Street in New York. The dance was held in the Hendrik Hudson ballroom filled with white cloth-covered dining tables and a big dance floor. Crewmembers and their wives or guests danced to the tunes of the day. The men wore their dark blue winter Navy uniforms and were happy to be celebrating among friends. The women didn't wear fancy dresses, but sported trendy little hats on their well-coiffed heads. Several officers in the crowd were wearing their Navy blazers with brass buttons and a shirt and tie.

Irma seemed troubled: *I am happy to be at the ship's party, but scared about what I know is coming*, she thought. As usual, Lou was enjoying the moment, looking like he didn't have a care in the world.

Two weeks later on October 26, the *Bull* left port and stopped in Norfolk, Virginia, to practice maneuvers with the Atlantic fleet's Amphibious Training Forces in Chesapeake Bay. After the ship departed Norfolk, it stopped in Pearl Harbor on November 7 to pick up crew for the Pacific War theater in the islands off the Philippines.

Even though Lou's brother-in-law had warned him about the brutality of war, Lou was not thinking of that as his ship departed New York. He may have been nervous about sailing so far away, but the sadness of leaving his family was foremost in his mind.

"I'm sure this war will be over soon, Irm," he wrote. "Until then, keep your spirits up."

October 26 (written in New York City)

Darling Husband of Mine: I kept thinking of you all day today. When I was coming home tonight from work, the moon was up in the sky already and I saw you on your ship in the dusky moonlight. It made me so sad.

I spoke to the [store] manager about leaving the store. He was very nice and very disappointed. He tried to make me stay in New

York for a while. You know my feelings towards this city, and now with you gone that goes a hundred times more!

However, I am staying until Saturday evening. So I'll be home in Cleveland sometime Sunday morning.

I have to close, I have a lot to do tonight. Dear, I'll be waiting for a call from you. I hope it shall be very soon.

—Sweet dreams, dear, Irma

November 1

Dearest Sweet One: We left Virginia November the 7th for Panama, got there Nov 12 on Sunday. There was only one liberty party and I got in on that. Tried to get you silk stockings, but there isn't any. They sure have everything else here like ice cream and bananas, coconuts. I sure had my fill of them.

Damn this heat, the sweat is just pouring off me. Wish you were here with me, dear. This Pacific Ocean is so peaceful and smooth and such a dark blue. It really is pretty. There are so many flying fish all over these waters. They jump out of the water and fly along-side of the ship. And there are sharks too, plenty of them, they just lay on the top of the water as we go by. Will close now, I have the 12:00 to 4:00 watch. Goodnight, sweet.

Hi! Sweet, here I am again. Well, every morning we have firing with all guns going. By the time I get to San Diego I will be hard of hearing. So when we were firing, we came under a cloudburst and did I get soaked. Can you picture me sitting by my gun and getting wet. Damn this heat, my sweat is getting this letter wet. That's all for now, will write more Saturday.

Well, here I am again, dear. Still at sea. The water is getting a bit rough now. There sure are a lot of sea turtles in the water, great big ones and little ones.

Saturday morning we did not fire at all. It looked like a storm was coming up. Sure enough, at night we hit it. Rain and spray was coming over the bow. Well, just before chow, I took a shower and put my clean pants and shorts on. Over the PA System came the orders, man your battle stations. So we did and, darling, did I get wet. It was raining and salt spray was all over me. Just as if someone was throwing buckets of salt water over me. I sit by my gun and that 5-inch gun is right in front of and below me. Every time it fired, the flash blinded me for a second or so.

Hi! Darling, back again with a little more news. We will be at the sea buoy [in San Francisco Harbor] tomorrow at 1400 hours, then only a couple of hours more we will be in San Francisco. Will call you the first chance I get. But it won't be until Wednesday, that is my liberty day.

They say women are always right. So I guess they are right. If that is true, please say I will come back in one piece. I always see you before me no matter what I seem to be doing. Have to close now, sweet, going on watch again.

—Good Night My Love

November 8

Dearest Lou: Darling, darling, I hope you have written many letters to me by this time.

I want so to hear from you. Please don't give me any excuses. That isn't what I want! Don't say there isn't anything to write about. There is too! Even if you just say things like "I got up from my chair and then sat down again." That's swell for me. It gives me a picture in my mind. I see you sitting. I see you standing. I picture you in the sun sitting! Or standing! Or in the rain standing! I see you sitting in the rain! (That's a very funny picture.) Can you see what I am driving at? Just that one sentence has given me at least five minutes of pictures of you.

So please write. Just anything! Everything you possibly say is important to me.

I love you so, dear, and am missing you much, dear.
—Goodnight, dear, Irma, Lola Lee & Diane

November 15

Dearest Lou: The girl's club is coming over here day after Thanksgiving. We are going to have a "Charm Party" that night. A cosmetic agent is coming here to show us the right way to put on make-up. For having the party at my house I'm going to get some cosmetics free ($2.00 or $3.00 worth). And get to look beautiful to boot. The only trouble with the whole thing is that you won't be here to see me glamorized!

The girls all say they are going to tell their husbands to stay up that night to see how nice they are made-up. And poor little me—what about me?

Darling, I still haven't heard from you. I hope something comes soon. Meantime, be good. Us three girls are. We are sending our love and kisses to the main man in our lives.

—Irma-Lola-Di

November 25

Dearest, Darling Irma: We left San Pedro [California] early Saturday morning. I am writing to you somewhere out on the Pacific. It is a little bit rough, but not like the North Atlantic. Over here it just has these long swells, makes the ship go up and down. You would think you are on a roller coaster. We sure need those sea legs when she starts to roll.

I wish now that you would have called Lola Lee to the phone so that I could have talked to the little doll and hear her voice for the last time. I guess you expected me to call you up again, sweet. but, after all, no sense of making it tough for both of us. It sure was grand to hear your voice again, darling. Wish to God I could call you up everywhere I go. Will close now, have the 4:00 to 12:00 watch.

—Goodnight, Hon

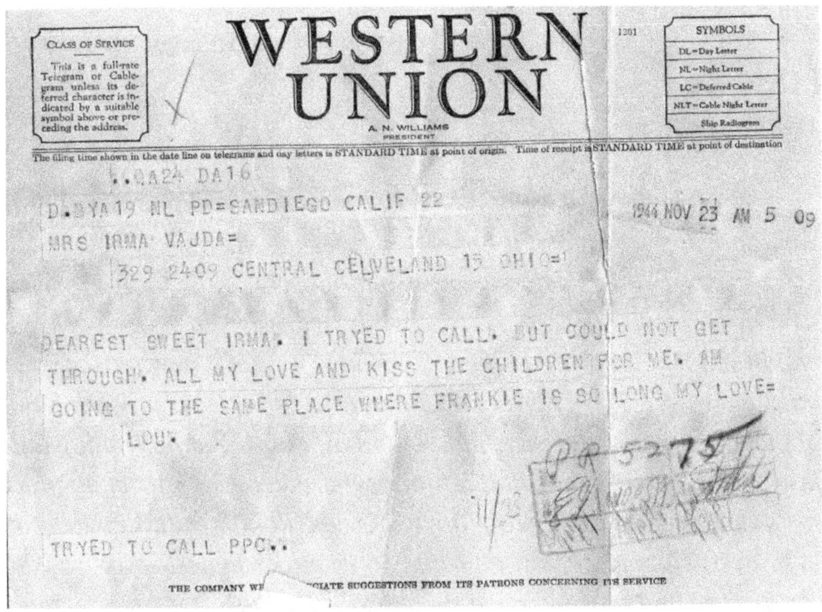

CLASS OF SERVICE
This is a full-rate Telegram or Cablegram unless its deferred character is indicated by a suitable symbol above or preceding the address.

WESTERN UNION
A. N. WILLIAMS
PRESIDENT

1201

SYMBOLS
DL=Day Letter
NL=Night Letter
LC=Deferred Cable
NLT=Cable Night Letter
Ship Radiogram

The filing time shown in the date line on telegrams and day letters is STANDARD TIME at point of origin. Time of receipt is STANDARD TIME at point of destination

..QA24 DA16
D.BYA19 NL PD=SANDIEGO CALIF 22 1944 NOV 23 AM 5 09
MRS IRMA VAJDA=
329 2409 CENTRAL CELVELAND 15 OHIO=

DEAREST SWEET IRMA. I TRYED TO CALL. BUT COULD NOT GET THROUGH. ALL MY LOVE AND KISS THE CHILDREN FOR ME. AM GOING TO THE SAME PLACE WHERE FRANKIE IS SO LONG MY LOVE=
LOU.

TRYED TO CALL PPC..

THE COMPANY W[...]CIATE SUGGESTIONS FROM ITS PATRONS CONCERNING ITS SERVICE

November 26

Dearest One: Today is Sunday so will write a few lines about last night. It was cold and windy, spray was coming over the ship, but I did not get too wet. They let us stay in the nearby clipping room [munitions compartment], leaving two men on watch for an hour and one-half, then two more of us would relieve them and so on.

And that moon was beautiful as I was looking at it. It made me wish that you could be at my side, dearest. But wishing would never make it so. Seeing that moon took me back to the times we had together in good old New York, even if we just went to a show. I will always remember the times we had no matter where I am.

I love you so, darling. And miss you just as you miss me. I will come back to you and the children, our married life cannot end this way. Do not worry or be afraid for me. I will be all right, sweet. Will take good care of myself for you. This is all I have to say today, so will close with love and kisses.

—So long my love

December 1

Hello Darling: As you can see, I missed one day in writing to you. So will try to make it up now.

I guess I didn't tell you that our mascot, Bull the dog, went AWOL (Absent Without Leave) while we were in New York. Or maybe somebody picked him up. Anyway, we got a new mascot, just a little pup yet. He's about three months old, cute as a baby. Some of the officers got together and bought him for the ship. But it would have been better if they had left him where he was. This is no place for a dog or even a man. So, anyway, we call him Bull, he bites like hell, even runs after you and bites one in the leg. He was seasick for a while, but now he's just an old salt. He has bit me many times, that's all I can say about him.

The weather is a lot warmer now, I've been standing watch. Wish you were here with me to enjoy this warm climate and that beautiful moon every night instead of going through another winter at home.

Darling, do you know this will be the second Christmas for me away from home and you? You bet I will think about you on Christmas day. Will write more as soon as I can think of something to say. So goodnight, dearest. Me loves you.

—Love to all, Lou

December 9

Dearest Lou: Well, it is just about three weeks before Christmas. And as usual I'm not ready. I'm trying to make too many of the gifts, I guess. Yet, if I don't, I really don't know how I'll ever manage to have money to buy gifts. Everything is about twice as much as last year.

I know you probably don't think I should even give any this year. But there are a few people you just must, because they insist on giving to you or yours.

I'm making both girls identical dresses that will be from you. I've been making doll clothes for two dolls, one for each of them that will be from me. Mom and Dad gave me $20.00 to spend on them and we've been buying toys. We got Lola a kitty-car, bunk beds for her dolls (by bunk bed I mean it's two beds one on top of the other with a ladder and all). I'm sure she'll like that, she's such a little mother. We are also looking for another doll buggy. I bought each of them big red stockings so they can hang them up the night before Christmas for Santa to fill. Only we haven't any fireplace, so shall have hang them on the living room radiator.

Mom also gave me $10.00 to buy something, but I think I'll wait and buy some shoes.

The money the children got from your parents I'm putting in the bank for them, $7.50 apiece.

I bought dad a bottle of liquor and I think I will get your dad the same.

I'm getting my mother odds and ends of wearing apparel and think I'll get your mom a couple aprons. Then, of course, I'll have the photos of each of the girls to give them.

Dear, darling, I hope this letter reaches you before the holidays. I want you to know just how we are spending it. Maybe we can pretend you are here with us. So think of us, darling, and be with us for we will be with you wherever you are. Besides, just think we are sure to be together next Christmas, and with each passing day it is just one day nearer.

So long, darling. God bless you and keep you. I hope you have a fairly good holiday.

—Love, Irma

December 20

Dearest Lou: Here it is almost Christmas and I'm behind as usual. But then it wouldn't be me if things were ready.

I made 5 clowns that cost $4.95 each at Taylor's [department store]. All five cost me about $1.00. I made a Humpty Dumpty for Lola, price $2.00 at the store, cost about $ .25. I also made a blouse for [my friend] that cost me $ .25 and would be about $5.00 at the stores.

Everything is about purchased. But everything has to be wrapped. Then too I have to trim the tree myself again this year...

Tomorrow I'd like to take Lola to see Santa Claus and the display windows in the department stores downtown. Stearn's [department store] has a cute one. Santa is taking a bath and his helpers are bringing his suit and pouring water in the tub and scrubbing his back. All the while he's laughing. I also want to take her to see Sterling and Welch's tree. They always have such a large one.

I should really have taken Lola down two or three times to take it all in.

You say in your last letter that I shouldn't let the children forget you. Darling, how could you! Lola talks about you every day. The choo-choo she hears is what you went away on. The boat in the magazine is what you are on. The sailor in the book she crayons is what you look like. At night she always kisses your picture and says goodnight to you. And even during the day when she passes your picture she goes to you and talks to you. I can't always make out what she says but it has something to do with

toys and candy. She talks to you on the telephone. I have had the operator ring me several times because Lola left the receiver off. So you can see you will always be mentioned and remembered day in and day out. You are here in our hearts. We all love you and miss you and want you back very, very soon.

—Goodnight Dear, Irma

Shopping in downtown Cleveland on Euclid Avenue easily rivaled the best shopping in the country, even New York City's Fifth Avenue. Six major department stores—Halle's, Higbee's, Sterling & Welch, the May Company, Bailey's, and Taylor's—provided a wealth of shopping choices. All the stores survived the Great Depression, and sales actually soared in the 1940s even with a war going on. All of the stores sold War Bonds during the war.

Irma enjoyed shopping in the department stores, especially when they introduced a new deferred payment plan whereby qualified customers had a specified amount of time from date of purchase to pay the balance due without incurring any additional charges. Higbee's opened the first bargain basement. Halle's was the first to install escalators (with wooden steps).

At the holidays, the stores provided an unmatched Christmas experience, beginning with large display windows themed and decorated to appeal to children. An annual holiday tradition for many families was to travel downtown to share the sights and marvel over the clever figures in the windows, often mechanically designed, like Santa Claus and his elves. Irma showed Lola all sixty-four of Higbee's decorated display windows.

Sterling & Welch, the oldest of all the stores, began a tradition of erecting a tall Christmas tree near the dining area covered with hundreds of lights and bulbs and dripping with shiny tinsel. Irma and Lola Lee stood at its base and gazed up at the glorious tree and oohed and ahhed. Of course, Lola visited Santa and Mrs. Claus too.

December 23

Dear Lou: I received your telegram this morning. There was so many, many things I wanted to tell you, ask you and everything. Why did this [postal] strike have to be just now? I guess that is just the way it had to be. No amount of "whys" will help. For that matter I've had "whys" on my mind ever since the war started.

All I'm worried about is whether you had turkey and what goes with it to eat. If you did, where did you have it, in port or on the ship? If not, what were you doing on November 23, 1944?

But next year, dear, we will celebrate together and I shall have turkey, stuffed to the gills and all the trimmings. And everything shall be just right. We will all sit down to this beautiful table with the turkey in the very center golden brown, and everything else all around steaming and throwing out their different odors. Then we shall give thanks and say this was a Thanksgiving Day. Until then there is no such thing for me or us or ours.

I looked up at the clean white sky this morning and I said to it, "Now, listen to me, fun is fun. And I appreciate a good joke as well as the next guy. I know we had to be shown. I know Lou had to be taught to get the Navy out of his system and that I had to learn a good many things such as to appreciate little things in life. But, really, you've let this thing go too far. We've learned our lesson. Darn good!"

—Good night my Darling, Dear Lou.
Kisses from all of us. Hugs too. Irma.

December 23

My Dearest Wife: Honey, you don't seem to write any mushy letters to me. I kind of miss letters like that. I should talk, my letters to you aren't so hot. I might as well learn how to write love letters or get a book about it. But I am trying, dear, will keep on trying as long as I live.

Well, I better close now or will go on and on with nothing more to say but how much I love you and miss you. I'm sorry, dear, but I can't tell you where I was or where we're going. But will say this much, when we get there, we will be halfway around the world, this crazy world of ours.

I hope next Christmas I will be home with all of you. We will have so much fun and do everything we didn't do before.

—I love you, Lou

December 26

Dearest Lou: Well, Christmas is over and things are more calm now. The tree is larger this year and much prettier. I still put it on the corner table in the middle of our window. It isn't quite as easy for the girls to reach the ornaments, although Lola is not having any trouble taking anything she wants off.

The shelf under the tabletop is full of presents for mom and dad. On the floor are the girl's toys, and all over the room for that matter. They have just loads of things. In fact, Lola can't decide what to play with.

I got money from mom, dad, and Chuck, $15.00 dollars in all. So I am plenty rich. But can't decide where to put it. There are so many things I would like to get. You know me.

—Love, Irma

December 27

Dearest Irma: Here we are anchored out in the harbor, it sure is pretty out here. The water is clear blue, if it wasn't so deep you could see the bottom. It's about four hundred eighty feet deep. We all went swimming as soon as we dropped the anchor, it sure was nice and warm. The deck was so hot we could have fried an egg on it. We have been taking salt showers on the bow of the ship or back aft. There was a shortage of fresh water for a while. But after all, that was better than nothing at all.

Other times as we were coming along and it would rain, some of us ran out to the back of the ship and took a freshwater shower. Darling, could you just picture me out there all naked taking a good rain shower? Boy, it sure was swell to wash down like that. And when it does rain, it just pours, just about everybody came out to wash down. Each one would wash the other fellow's back. It's too bad you weren't the one to wash my back for me. Maybe one of these days you will do it for me, hon. Hope that day isn't far off, keep your chin up, sweet, before you know I will be home for good.

It's hot as hell during the day and nice and cold in the evening. Not always cool below but topside its just right. Just came back from the ship store with some good candy, I am eating while I'm writing to you. It sure is good to have candy way out here.

Darling, you should see how beautiful it is out here at night. There are so many stars out. Billions of them, they twinkle so.

This is all dear, I have the 8:00 to 12:00 watch, so I say good-night, sweetheart, until we meet tomorrow.

—Love to all, Lou

December 29

My Dearest One: Had to miss one day of writing to you. The reason was that we went swimming yesterday, and fishing too, did not have any luck, though. It sure is hard swimming out here, the current is pretty strong. At times I have to swim like hell to get back to the side of the ship. Wish we could go on the beach, it would be more fun if we could, but that's impossible to do. Will tell you the reason why some day.

Just heard that we will be here until after New Year's. Then we leave for our destination, from there on the fireworks will really start. But don't you worry about me, darling. Just keep on loving me, darling, and thinking about me, for I will be doing the same thing, sweet.

—So long, dearest, Lou, Love to all, Love to all

Chapter 5

1945, Winter: Miss You So Much

January 2

Dearest Lou: It seems rather queer writing 1945. But then it does every year when the year changes. Anyway, I'm glad I don't have to write 1944 anymore. 1944 has been a very disappointing year for me—us. The one joy it gave us was the new baby. And ok! Yes, my being with you in New York [on your leaves]. While there were great joys in my life, I expected bigger things of 1944, like the war being over and you boys being back with us. So now I expect these big things of 1945 and I do hope I won't be disappointed. I feel in my bones I won't be. I hope I am right.

What were you doing New Year's Eve? I spent it at mother's reading a book, only stopping long enough to wish you a "Happy New Year." I said a small prayer too. It wasn't a long prayer because I know He was listening overtime anyway, because I know many, many people were saying prayers too.

The children are fine. Lola has two more teeth upfront.

—Love, Irma

When the *Bull* arrived in Pearl Harbor its orders were to transport members of UDT #14 to the Palau Islands and then to nearby Ulithi Islands. This would be the staging area for the invasion of Luzon Island in the Philippines. According to Navy records,

Luzon Island was the USS *Bull's* first engagement in the Pacific War. It lasted from January 6 to January 11.

While sailing in the Lingayen Gulf off Luzon, the convoy of 63 or more ships came under repeated attacks from hundreds of Japanese suicide bombers. The Japanese Zero or kamikaze pilots were young men trained to crash into enemy ships with their cargo of bombs—they would not return home. At one point, a plane crashed 20 yards off the side of the *Bull*; later a bomb was dropped 200 yards off the deck, but the ship and crew were not hurt.

While returning to its base, the *Bull* also helped to rescue a Navy pilot who had ditched in the sea off the Philippine coast.

January 10 (V-Mail)

Dearest Sweet Lou: We are doing fine and hope the same is true with you. It has been about zero degrees around here for some time. It also keeps snowing on and off. The streets are never clean and snow keeps piling up. If you want to get on a bus or something you have to wade through snow to the center of the street. Once the buses get in the pile of snow they have to be pushed out. It's really something.

I love you dear. I miss you very much—Irma

V-Mail or Victory Mail was developed by Eastman Kodak during the war to give enlisted men an alternative method to write home. Unlike Air Mail letters that were bulky to transport, and required a longer time to reach their destination, V-Mails were censored at the various Naval fleet post offices—San Francisco, New York, Chicago—and transferred to microfilm before being flown to key locations in the European and Pacific theatres for processing. The microfilm negatives were blown up to 60 percent of their original size using Kodak's photography equipment, printed, and distributed to the sailors. This new letter delivery method became very popular as the war progressed.

Because of their small size, 4 inches by 5 inches, V-Mails, like postcards, provided less space for messages—love letters had to be brief. They acted as both stationery and envelope and were provided free of charge to servicemen and their wives.

Lou didn't like to use V-Mail and wrote very few. Irma, on the other hand, appreciated the ability to dash off a quick note every day, in addition to the longer letters she mailed via the fleet post office.

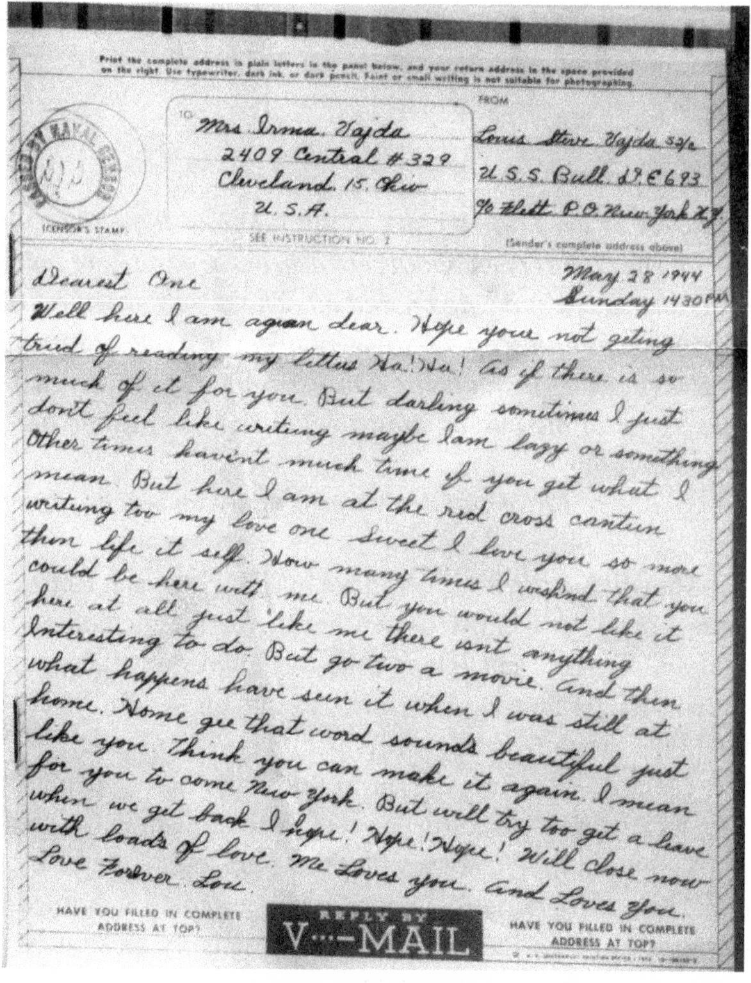

Print the complete address in plain letters in the panel below, and your return address in the space provided on the right. Use typewriter, dark ink, or dark pencil. Faint or small writing is not suitable for photographing.

TO: Mrs Irma Vajda
2409 Central #329
Cleveland. 15. Ohio
U.S.A.

FROM: Louis Steve Vajda S2/c
U.S.S. Bull. D.E 693
c/o Fleet P.O. New York N.Y.

(CENSOR'S STAMP) SEE INSTRUCTION NO. 2 (Sender's complete address above)

Dearest One
May 28 1944
Sunday 1430 PM

Well here I am again dear. Hope you not geting tired of reading my letters Ha! Ha! As if there is so much of it for you. But darling sometimes I just don't feel like writing maybe I am lazy or something. Other times haven't much time if you get what I mean. But here I am at the red cross canteen writing too my love one. Sweet I love you so more then life it self. How many times I wished that you could be here with me. But you would not like it here at all just like me there isnt anything interesting to do. But go two a movie. And then what happens have seen it when I was still at home. Home gee that word sounds beautiful just like you. Think you can make it again. I mean for you to come New York. But will try too get a leave when we get back I hope! Hope! Hope! Will close now with loads of love. Me Loves you. And Loves You. Love Forever. Lou

HAVE YOU FILLED IN COMPLETE ADDRESS AT TOP?

REPLY BY V···–MAIL

HAVE YOU FILLED IN COMPLETE ADDRESS AT TOP?

January 14

My Dearest Wife: Oh, my darling, it seems so long since I have heard from you. Hoping to have some news from you when I get back to where we started. Maybe I'll get those packages that you told me about too.

I sure have seen a lot of everything already, it's nothing to write about though. It isn't pleasant even to talk about it much less to write about.

Still keeping your chin up, dear? Don't let it get you down, hon. This will be over before you know it. And when that day comes, dear, I will send a telegram saying what day I will arrive and then you and my two little loves will meet me at the station. That, my darling, will be the happiest day in our lives. To see all of you again and forever after, that is what I am living for, waiting for. Fighting for.

The last place where we were you should have seen this tiger shark in the harbor where we were anchored. It came right up to the ship on the port side. It must have been 15 feet long or better. When it opened its mouth, man, what saw-like teeth it had. When the captain saw it, he said there would be a swimming party for all hands on the fantail. That was a good laugh for all of us.

Just got through with chow, we had chicken but not like the way your mother makes it or my mother, with dumplings and all the trimmings.

I heard there was a cold spell [back there], was it bad or not? Out here it's hot as hell as I always said. Am sweating so much every day that my tan is coming right off with the sweat. It has been so hot below decks that I have been sleeping topside. Sometimes I take my mattress up with me, other times just use my jacket to lie down on. It's so warm that even the steel deck is enough [to keep me warm]. I always sleep near my gun, so am always ready when GQ [General Quarters] sounds.

—Loving you always, Lou

January 15 (V-Mail)

My Dearest Wife: I thought I would write one of these [V-Mail] letters for a change. The weather is pretty hot today, as usual I am sweating away.

The sky is a pretty blue just like the water, with flying fish jumping out and flying around. We are just passing a few rocky islands, they sure look good to me—the good old earth.

When we get back to where we started from we are going to have a beach beer party, wish you could be with me now and have a beer or two on the beach. But you and I will do that together one of these days.

Well, darling, we went through our first naval engagement with flying colors. Shot down a suicide bomber that was trying to get us. But we beat him to the punch. Boy! It was sure nice to see him hit the water. Yep! We are one tough crew and that goes for my ship too. She is one swell little ship. After all, she is my home now and we have to take care of her for she does the same. So this is all for now, sweet, until we get to port. I love you.

—Good night dearest, Lou

January 16 (V-Mail)

Dearest Lou: I wrote you a nice long letter yesterday. But I don't think you'll get it as fast as this one (being V-Mail).

I got a War Bond from the Navy Department today. That is three you bought since you signed up for it.

I received a Xmas card from you last week, but no letters. What's up?

—Love, Irma

P.S. Hugs and kisses from the kids.

To finance the military operations of the most expensive war in U.S. history—the cost was more than $300 billion—the U.S. Treasury began selling a series of war bonds to its citizens after the attack on Pearl Harbor. Lou must have been encouraged by his superiors to buy them, as he owned three by January 1945.

Sold in increments as low as $25 up to $10,000, the bonds paid the very low rate of return of 2.9 percent, maturing ten years after the date issued. A $25 bond cost $18.75 upfront or 75 percent of its face value.

The government launched an epic advertising campaign to urge the public to purchase war bonds, appealing to their love of country. Americans were also reminded that bonds were a safe investment for their savings on the heels of the economic uncertainties created by the Great Depression.

Radio, newspaper, and magazine ads were designed by leading ad agencies of the era. Some media provided free space, other companies designed ads to show their patriotism. The ads provided a strong emotional appeal with illustrations of babies, children, and wounded soldiers. After the battle of Iwo Jima, the famous photo of the Marines raising the U.S. flag on Mount Suribachi proved to be effective in selling bonds. The soldiers in the photo were sent on a goodwill public relations tour around the country to promote war bond sales. Film celebrities and entertainers also donated their time to travel the country putting on shows for the troops and selling bonds.

January 18 (V-Mail)

Dear Lou: I hope and pray things are going smoothly for you. It is hard for me to wait for your letters. But I suppose when I do get some there will be many. I do hope your mail is reaching you. I wouldn't want you to be without mail as long as I have here.

Love, Irma

January 20 (V-Mail)

Dear Husband of Mine: I hate Saturday night, people coming and going in each of the other apartments.

Dear Lou, I wish you were around. I'd talk your ear off. I'm sure you'd understand. I want you here with me. I just can't begin to realize how far away you are from me. Think of us always, darling, as we do of you.

—Kisses & Hugs from all your girls, Irma

January 21

Dear Lou: Today being Sunday, it's also my long letter day to you. Of course, I write you V-Mails the same as every other day.

Boy, I sure have been catching up on my letter writing since my [New Year's] resolution. Did I tell you what it was? Well, I made up my mind I would write you a V-Mail every day and also a letter to some one. On Saturdays and Wednesdays I write to my brother. On Sundays a long letter to you. It really only leaves four other days a week for my other letters. I started with the person I haven't written in the longest time and work my way up. The first letter was to [your brother] Johnny. What do you think of my program? Good, huh? If I stick to it.

Darling, don't be hurt that I only send you a small V-Mail each day. If I had to write a long letter every day I'd sure stop my fine program before long because really sometimes it's hard for me to finish even a small letter to you. Then too, I'd only repeat myself each day and even at that wouldn't have enough to write you. V-Mails go faster to you also, and you can always find time to read them, whereas if it was a long letter full of things you've heard of before you'd maybe never even finish reading it. What do you think of V-Mails anyway?

Mom and Dad always tell me to mention them to you. They say "Hello" too. Of course they always ask of you and want to know how you are doing. As if I know.

Dear darling, how I wish you could be here with us and experience these little [family] moments with us. To laugh over them or cry over them as the case may be. I feel like I'm only half this way. Nothing can I laugh at wholeheartedly or for that matter ever cry fully. It seems like all my feelings are only half and never full. It is such a terrible thing to go through. Can you know what I mean?

—Darling, Love-Love-Love From your little Boss—Irma
Hugs and kisses from your daughters

January 25 (V-Mail)

Dearest Darling Lou: I was hoping you weren't in any of the fights, but I see that's not so. Now I'm trying to figure which one you were in, Luzon? Or Formosa? Or the one along the China coast? Maybe not one of those. What does it matter as long as it is one step towards home. Oh, my sweet, sweet darling, I can't imagine what it will be like to meet you at the station and to hear your home for good.

—Love, Irma

January 26

Dearest Sweet Irma: Arrived here the 23 [of January], next day I got your letter dated Dec. 20, it sure took a long time to get here. It sure was wonderful to hear from you and to know that everything is alright with you and the kids. Yesterday I received your two V-Mail letters. So now I am twice as happy as before. And to know that our little children still think of me and talk about me, I am so proud of you, darling, to teach the children not to forget their Sailor Daddy. Today, [the weather] isn't so bad, though it has been raining since this morning. And when it rains here, it just pours. Like last night I slept topside as always, the rain woke me up but I just wrapped the blanket close around me and kept right on sleeping. It's so nice to sleep topside with all the pretty stars twinkling above me and that moon looking down at me. I always look at the moon and say goodnight to all of you. When I am saying that to you it is daylight where you're at. In fact, we are a day ahead of you. So when I say goodnight you are just getting up.

So you had a hard time before the holidays, darling, sewing and everything for the kiddies and for everybody. You must have been very tired afterward.

Those packages you said you sent me, I didn't receive yet. Still hoping though that I will get it. I would like to taste more of those cookies that you make, yes, darling, I sure miss those good cookies that you make, your mother's too.

I just can't put it in writing anymore or say how much I love you. For I was meant for you and you were meant for me. When I get home for good, dear, I never will let you out of my sight. Wherever I go, you will go. We will be together forever and ever.

Hoping that more letters will come before we pull out of here and start knocking the hell out of those crazy Japs again. Enclosed is some Japanese money that I picked up at the last place we were.

I also have some pretty seashells that you could put on a dress or make a necklace out of. Am trying to get a box to mail them to you. They are really pretty, all kinds of colors and they shine like a diamond.

—Loving you always, Lou

January 29 (V-Mail)

Dear Lou: I went to a movie tonight. Saw "Meet Me in St. Louis" at the State [theater].

It was cute and had nice coloring on it. Judy Garland played in it. Also Margaret O'Brien that child star. The whole thing suited

my mood nicely and it had nothing about war in it. It is nice not to remember even for an hour. Of course, you never completely forget. For you always feel things are not right, but for those few minutes you at least forget. Will we ever be able to wake up and feel completely right with the world? Some day we will, I suppose. All things must end sooner or later.

How are you dear? I hope things aren't too hard for you. And please don't think we don't know how hard it is for you. Of course, we can't realize completely but we do know a little of what it must be like for you. If I knew completely, I wouldn't bear it, I'm sure. This way at least I can imagine it not being as hard.

—Irma & Lola-Diane

Irma was particularly upset by the violence in war movies and eventually chose not to attend. However, she was anxious to see the newsreels that accompanied the feature films because they helped her to track the war's progress and Lou's whereabouts. If she wanted more up-to-date information about the battles, she stopped at Telenews Theatre on Euclid Avenue that had an all-newsreel format. They also posted war bulletins on the marquee.

The 1940s proved to be the golden years for movie attendance. Motion pictures, along with radio, were the major form of entertainment and escapism for Americans. Large viewing spaces like nickelodeons and movie theatres were able to present movies longer in length, and soon double features were shown with newsreels of current events plus cartoons for the kids. Family members were able to make a night of watching movies together, especially when refreshments were sold too. During the war, Irma had a regular movie-going night, sometimes with friends but often alone.

"Sometimes I stayed to see the same movies over again," Irma said after the war. "I wanted more time to forget about the war. Ma was at home with the kids and would worry that something bad had happened to me." Irma expressed some guilt about taking advantage of her mother's kindness, but she didn't change her ways.

Early in the war, movies based on real occurrences were produced with happy endings for an audience wishing to escape the realities of wartime. Musicals like *Yankee Doodle Dandy* (1942) and *Meet Me in St. Louis* (1944) were popular with the home front and GIs. Even Gen. Dwight Eisenhower, while planning the Normandy invasion in 1944, urged Hollywood: "Let's have more motion pictures."

In 1944 the movie-going public topped 85 million a week, about 60 percent of the U.S. population; tickets cost 32 cents. Lonely war wives and servicemen both used movies to temporarily forget about the stresses of everyday life, immersing themselves in the Humphrey Bogart and Lauren Bacall feature *To Have and Have Not (*1944) or the Spencer Tracy flick *Thirty Seconds Over Tokyo* (1944).

As the war dragged on and casualties increased, the public tired of war movies. Films became more honest and realistic, like *Objective Burma* (1945) with Errol Flynn and *The Story of GI Joe* (1945) with Burgess Meredith and Robert Mitchum. By the time the war ended in 1945, attendance had increased to 90 million a week. A number of movies were released that showed the effects on families and society when wounded soldiers returned home: *The Best Years of Our Lives* won the Academy Award for Best Picture in 1946.

In addition to their entertainment value movies during the war years had an outsized effect on American life and culture. A host of fan magazines, like *Photoplay* and *Modern Screen,* were very popular with teens and women, as were fan clubs. Movies and movie stars influenced adult fashions and fed housewives' romantic yearnings while shaping the social behaviors of the teen culture.

February 6

My Dearest Wife: Yes, darling, everything is going all right with me, here's hoping that everything is going smoothly for you. I always told you not to worry about me for I'm taking good care of myself. So you just take care of yourself and not worry anymore... But you can bet your sweet life I will come home just as soon as they say, here, Vajda, are your papers, I will catch the fastest train for home or if possible, the first plane. And I will fly right into those loving arms of yours and stay there the rest of my life.

Glad to hear your club is still going strong, at least you have some place to go to get together with girls your own age. How well I remember when I took you to your Friday Club meeting and came for you later in our little car. I wonder where it is now? I suppose if I was home now I wouldn't be taking you to your club meeting because I would be staying at home taking care of the kids. That sure would be swell...that sure would be heaven taking care of my two little girls and playing with them. And that is another reason you or I will never grow old, not with those two little dolls around us. So my little girl doesn't like to stay in her playpen, do you remember Lola Lee was just like that...Bless her little heart, she is so sweet just like her darling mother....

Just got through drinking a cup of Joe, it sure was good. In case you don't know, that means coffee.

For some reason we can't go swimming out here...But then I really don't mind because it kind of gets me at times, it's so deep. I should say about 80 feet or better and the current is pretty strong. One fellow got pulled out quite a ways, so we had to send a boat out after him.

Well, this is all for tonight, sugar....

—Love & Kisses to all three of you, Lou

P.S. I love you very much.

Try and get me some film, 120 Kodak

Every battle in the Pacific War was crucial to victory for the Allies, but the fight for the islands of Iwo Jima and Okinawa were especially critical because of their importance as a staging area for the planned attack on Japan. The *Bull* was part of a massive military plan called Operation Iceberg to secure the two Japanese islands. All told, 450 ships took part in securing Iwo Jima.

On February 10, the *Bull's* convoy headed to Iwo Jima, 660 miles south of mainland Japan, and assisted UDT #14 in its mission to scout the island for the planned invasion on February 19. The *Bull* also provided firepower support and cover in the UDTs' effort to clear the beaches for the Marines tasked with securing the island in order to build U.S. airfields. The ship came under Japanese fire many times, but was not damaged despite several near misses. When the island was captured on March 16, the total destruction and loss of life were enormous. U.S. forces lost more than 7,000 Marines; 20,000 were wounded. Japanese losses numbered close to 18,000 soldiers.

Lou was very proud of his gun crew on Gun #41, calling them "the best shooting crew aboard ship." He had a photo taken with his friend Lovas standing in front of the ship's guns, "The Two Hungarians."

The *Bull's* crew saw the historic raising of the American flag by a team of Marines on 550-foot high Mount Suribachi on February 23. The Battle of Iwo Jima made a lasting impression on American consciousness because of its ferocity. The image of six Marines struggling to plant the U.S. flag was immortalized in a photo snapped by Associated Press photographer Joe Rosenthal, and later cast in bronze by Navy sculptor Felix W. de Weldon.

February 6 (V-Mail)

Dear Hubby: I went downtown [Cleveland] today to the Stillman [theater] and saw Til We Meet Again. I believe you saw it, I can't remember if you liked it or not. I like it very much. Although, I don't usually like war pictures anymore. That is to say it isn't that I dislike war pictures, but I don't let myself go see them. I'm with the war every part of the day and night other times.

You should see downtown at night now. Even when they are open evenings, the window lights aren't burning [because of the blackout regulations]. The movie signs are out too. Everything looks like it's closed until you are in front of the doors, then you can see the lights inside. Also, everything is dead on Mondays all day. Even more so than it used to be on Sundays. For even the shows are closed, and restaurants. It is the least we back home can do.

—Love, Irma

February 18

Dearest Lou: Today I took my wedding suit out. Remember it, dear? I am making that wedding suit of mine over to wear it [for] Easter. You remember it was a dress and jacket with fur on it. Well, I'm making a skirt and jacket without fur. I can make a couple more blouses and no one would know it is almost five years old.

Dear darling of mine, after much studying of maps I have decided your ship base is Guam. There has been much talk here that we may invade Formosa and I thought perhaps you'd been in on it. But since then Iwo Jima Island in the volcano group have been reported invaded and I feel even as I write you may be in heavy battle. For the radio has just given out the news and they say there is a strong battle going on. Of course, I keep hoping I am wrong and that you aren't in it. There was no talk of Marines on the invasion of Luzon so you must have taken in the Army. But there is not much talk of Marines in the invasion of Iwo Jima so that is what it must have been this time. Of course, this may and probably is all wrong. Maybe some day you can tell me, I can wait.

The sun was out today. But it was cold. And yet it makes you feel better just to see that good old sun out. And then too you can see patches of green grass and you can begin to hope that some day soon it will be spring and warm again.

Darling, I've been so lonesome for you over this weekend. Anyway, I just can't stand Sunday anymore. There isn't any mail delivery and I have nothing to look forward to. And Monday morning always seems so far away.

Oh darling, I hope you are well and may God watch over you.

—Love forever—Irma & the children

On March 5 the *Bull* departed from Iwo Jima with its task force and returned to its base, where they held firing practice with Lou's gun crew. On March 25, the *Bull* steamed to Okinawa, 360 miles south of mainland Japan, with 92 members of UDT #14 onboard prepared to launch amphibious operations. Kamikaze attacks by Japanese Zero pilots increased significantly as Allied forces closed in on the Japanese islands.

"Those crazy Japs," Lou wrote later. "They tried to fly their planes right into our ships in Okinawa harbor. They flew low and came real close, but we took them out."

Okinawa was invaded on April 1 and the ferocious battle continued for approximately 80 days. The formidable effort to take the island from Japanese forces was complicated by the network of tunnels the Japanese had dug into the island's coral limestone. The Japanese troops had hunkered down in a 60-mile-long bunker that circled the island until Allied troops employed flamethrowers to flush them out. In all, 12,000 American and 77,000 Japanese soldiers were killed. The Japanese also lost 1,465 pilots and planes while defending Okinawa; 33 Navy ships were damaged or sunk. The Battle of Okinawa secured the course of the war and the eventual surrender of the Japanese.

The *Bull* spent three additional months off Okinawa providing beach reconnaissance and screening of Allied ships until the island was cleared of final Japanese resistance on June 22.

The horrors of these two battles were revealed to the home front in newsreels and radio news bulletins. Lou was unable to describe his circumstances or share his feelings about what he was seeing with Irma because of the censorship rules. At some point during these two battles, Lou lost his shipboard buddy. In spite of this, the few letters he was able to write home depicted life on board the ship as usual with little mention of the emotional tension and danger he was experiencing. At home, fear and anxiety grew for wives and families with husbands, fathers, sons or brothers in the battles.

March 11, South Pacific

Dearest Irma: I don't remember ever telling you that we always have watches to stand whether we're underway or at anchor, so tonight it is my turn, and then will be off for three days. And so on down the line. So let me tell you how it is out here at night.

There are several small islands where we're at, this has been our base right along. But what I wanted to say is that at night it's so pretty out here. All the ships have some of their lights on so that to me it just looks like a small town on top of the water. But then in the morning everything is spoiled because all I can see is just ships and water and more water. [At night] it reminds me of the time when you and I went on a moonlight ride [around Lake Erie] and we could see all the lights from the shore.

I received 7 V-Mail letters from you today. I'm so happy tonight that I finally heard from you and the children are in good health. I still have this head cold of mine but I think by the time you get this letter I will have sweated it out. I wish I could send some of this warm weather home to you like you ask in one of your letters. I'm fed up with all this heat everyday, only time it's nice and cool is at night and then only if a person stays topside. Wishing you were here at my side now to see all this pretty scenery that is around here.

—Loads of love to all, Big Boss

March 11

Dearest Lou: Today we heard on the radio that Mindanao [an island in the Philippines] has been invaded. So I'm all mixed up again. I now wonder if you are in on that. Although it isn't as likely as Iwo Jima was. The only thing that is making me uncertain is that if you were in the Iwo Jima invasion you should be back at your base by this time and I should be hearing from you. Of course, I did get those letters dated Feb 12-14, but that was written before your mission unless you mailed those as soon as you got back at the base. Well, maybe Monday I'll get two together again.

Darling, you read so many stories and hear them over the radio where men coming back from the service find it hard to get into the family again. That the wife finds it hard to get close to him again. What I want to say, dear, is that I never had that feeling and I don't have it now. You are always close to me and I always feel that oneness even as far away as you are. Do you think, dear, that maybe you'll find it hard to be with us again? I don't think you'll say you will, but I'd like to know for sure. Be honest.

Forgive me if I don't make sense, but I am in earnest and must know.

—Love darling, Irma

March 12 (V-Mail)

Dearest Lou: Today being Monday and my day or night out, I went to a movie again. I saw "Objective: Burma" with Errol Flynn. I don't like him, but the picture was good. Although there weren't any girls or romance in it, and you know I just have to have romance in my movies. But this picture was very, very interesting. I learned a lot. I'm sure you'd like it too, I hope you see it. But since you only get old pictures on the ship, I hope the war is over before it reaches your ship.

I bought mom a set of dinner dishes for 12. It is her birthday next Saturday and dad and I are giving that as a gift. I know she'll appreciate it more than anything else we could have gotten her. It is really nice, it has a silver design around the outer edge and a light blue line about half-inch wide a little further in. It cost $30.00. I think dad and I are going "halfsies" on it. It is more than I can afford but mom does deserve it. She is always doing something for us. And she spends a lot more on my birthdays than that.

The children are well, cutting more teeth but it doesn't seem to bother them.

—Love, Irma

Irma bought her mother her first set of matching dishes. They were not fine china, but they were the only set of dishes her mother ever owned. They were used for birthday celebrations and holiday gatherings. Memories of the sights and smells of food are strong in most families. These dishes were associated with rich chicken noodle soup made by Irma's mother. The serving platter held the turkey at Thanksgiving and strudel at anytime of the year. Holiday dinners were particularly bittersweet for Irma because they emphasized her feeling of aloneness from others celebrating with their husbands.

"I wish Lou could have been home with us this past holiday season," she said to her mother. "He *has* to be home this year! I hope and pray all the boys will be home. The war must be over by then!"

March 13, South Pacific

Dearest Irma: It's so hot out here. I really believe we could fry an egg on the deck. The water is a pretty deep blue, but we can't see fishes around here, we aren't even fishing or swimming at all, for one reason, the current is too strong.

So when I don't have anything to do, I read a book or write to you. I would sooner sit down and write to you, dearest, for it makes me feel so good. For I know when you hear from me it makes you happy. I always want you to be very happy, darling. Sometimes [your letters] are kind of sad, don't feel that way, hon, for it makes me feel the same way then.

I get lonesome and blue lots of times, so what I do is just think of you and the children and it picks me right up. (Remainder of letter lost]

March 15, South Pacific

Dearest V-Mail Irma: Today for chow we had a nice piece of ham but it wasn't enough for me so now am eating some of your good cookies. Boy, they sure are good, all the fellows like them. They all say what a swell cook you are.

I see by your letter that the kids are keeping you on the run, those little devils of mine. Darling, I'd just about give anything to be home with the kids and you to see my little girls growing up the way they are now, for am really missing the best part of their lives. Well, dear, you asked me in your last letter if I was at that place. So you guessed right, hon. I was there and it was hell while it lasted. That's all I can say just now. Besides, I'm sure you wouldn't want to hear all of it.

I'm so happy to hear that Lola is able to speak those words already, to think she says dada and mama to you. Bless the little doll, for that's what she seemed to me when I left.

So, that's what's worrying you, is it? Because [our friends separated], that would never happen to us, darling, for we have much to live for. Furthermore, don't compare us with them for we have so much in common and such two sweet little girls, as everybody says.

Darling, do you or can you just imagine us ever doing anything like that after all the hell we've been through. No, I can't. We will be happy, dear, as we were before we argued about the least little things. Those arguments didn't mean a thing for they were just love spats. I haven't just married you for your looks alone. I married you for what you are, a wonderful sweet little mother for those two adorable girls that you have brought into this world and to us.

So will close now with loads of love, kisses to all, Salty Lou

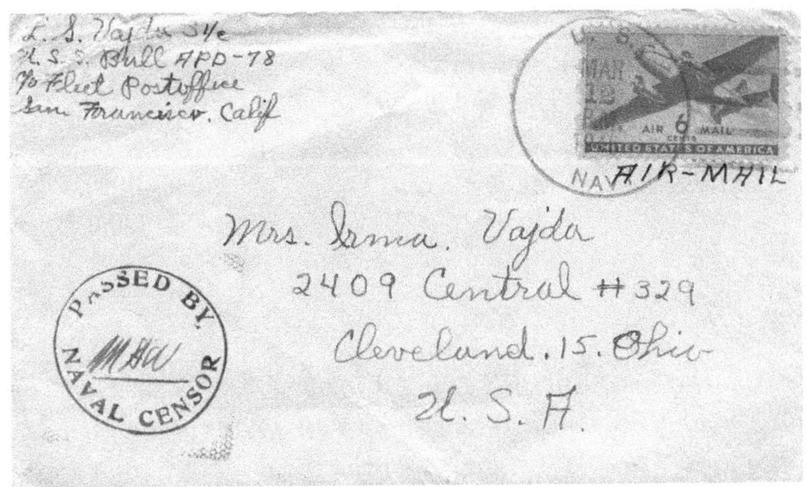

March 16, South Pacific

Dearest Irma: I received your letter of January 29 two days ago, kind of late. No wonder, you only had a three-cent stamp on it. So next time, please send it airmail like I do. You never did tell me how long it takes before you get one of my letters.

It's raining like hell topside, so they are going to show the movie in the mess hall. There will be two showings because we can't all fit in at once. So maybe I'll go to the second one, if I didn't see it already.

In your letter, you say you are going to send me a photo. All right. Keep your word now, and send it as fast as you can. Darling, I miss your picture, so the one of both you and me isn't big enough.

I really don't have much to say so I will answer your letter. I have the same thoughts about you too, what you are doing, how you are doing, where you go, and oh, so many things. I often wonder how I would look again in civilian dress. I sure would like to wear those nice clothes again. And when that day does come around (and I come home), hon, you and I will go out together and you can pick out some nicer clothes for you and me, then we'll really step out.

So my little [Lola] Lee is always writing me a letter, that would really be something if she could. Bless her little heart. I love her so and miss her little laugh. Tell her that her daddy will bring her something home or will send it by mail.

God Bless all of you, my dear, and watch over you for me. Goodnight, darling. Me loves you.

—I love you so. Salty Lou

March 21 (V-Mail)

Dearest Lou: Am still sewing. Finished the blouse. Looks nice but probably won't last long. I made it out of one of my old dresses and I didn't realize just how poor the material was until I had it started. But I always did like the print and therefore must just use it up.

If you remember it was the dress over which we had a fight before we were married. Foolish me. Little did we know back then the big things that were going to happen in our lives. It is too bad we spent even a minute being unhappy now that we have so much of it.

—I love you sweet patient love of mine, Irma

March 25

To My Salty Lou: I'm so happy this weekend, dear. I got three swell letters from you.

So you finally got a couple of my packages. Good! Those two packages were to be for Valentine's Day. Kind of late, huh? But there are three packages to be accounted for before those you got.

They were to be your Christmas gifts, two of them. The other one was the work pants and shirt I wrote you I would send because you asked your [sister] Margaret for them. I think the first two were sent to the New York address and that is the delay.

I haven't missed your letters at all, darling, so if you are missing one or two here and there, they are just lost or else the censors didn't like them. And you know I'm not sure what displeases the censors.

Oh, darling, how we all miss you and how we all want you at home. Dear, God bless you and bring you home safe to us soon. Love from us all.

—To my Big Boss from "Little Boss"

March 26 (V-Mail)

Dearest Lou: I saw "Hotel Berlin" today with Faye Cameron and some other stars. The picture itself wasn't to my taste. If you saw it, you would know why.

Darling, I got three more letters from you this morning. And each one had a check in it. I nearly fell over. Thank you, dear, I think I'll do the same as I did with the other, put $70.00 in the bank bringing our account to $140.00, and I'll use the $10.00 for something for the house this time. I'll let you know what I do with it when I do it.

Oh yes, of the $10.00 from the first time, I bought two books for each girl tonight, at $1.25 apiece and two pairs of hose each to match their new dresses for Easter. The books are nursery rhymes and Mother Goose stories. I'll read them each a bedtime story and a little poem. They are getting old enough for things like that. They can always have these books even when they are parents themselves to read to their children. Oh my! Now I'm making us grandparents, I'd better stop!

—Love, Irma & the children

March 31 (V-Mail)

Dearest Lou: We are all ready for Easter here tomorrow. Mom and dad are coming for us early in the morning. Mom wanted to take Lola Lee home with her this afternoon, but I wouldn't let Lola go. I want Lola and Diane to wake in the morning together in their own home and see and enjoy together what the Easter bunny brought them.

I wish you could get a glance of the living room. There are two little undershirts set out, one on one section of the sofa, the other on another one, side by side. There's a diaper besides the smallest shirt, a pair of panties besides the larger shirt. Then each section has a blue dress laid out on it. Two white hair ribbons fixed with bobby pins and all. A navy coat and hat hanging on the playpen and a blue knitted coat and bonnet alongside of it. Two little pairs of white shoes are drying under the radiator, polished white and clean. On each side of the radiator on the floor is an Easter basket and Easter stuffed bunny (from your mother), and gaily-wrapped packages contain some books and colored eggs. Yes, everything is in readiness for Easter morning. So I think I'll turn in.

—Goodnight, my dear, Irma

April 1

Darling Lou: How are you dear husband of mine? Where are you today? What are you doing? Are you thinking of us even as we are of you?

I am worried there has been another large invasion in the Pacific. Okinawa? But you can't be in all the invasions, besides your letters haven't said anything of going out again. Well, I'll know if I don't get any more letters this coming week that you are out of your base again.

Easter day was pretty nice. The children looked cute dressed in their very best. We took some "snaps." If they come out I'll send them right away.

We colored two dozen eggs this year, one for mom and one for us. They were pretty nice. Lola got ours at home the first hour she was up in the morning and crushed about half of them. She thought that was great fun. So what to do?

My suit came out pretty good too. I feel good in it and that is the acid test you know. The blouse looks good too. All in all, everything was ok. But Easter evening is such a letdown. You buy, prepare, and look forward to Easter so long in advance and then "bingo," the day is over with. Why all the fuss, I wonder?

We had traditional ham for dinner and potato salad besides the side dishes, also had [Hungarian] nut rolls for dessert and Jell-O. Are you much interested? I guess not!

Mom and dad bought a house last week. It was all done in such a hurry I never had a chance to see it. They took me down this afternoon to see it, and I don't like it. But dad was in such a hurry and it was supposed to be such a bargain. The house itself is not bad, fairly decent looking. It's a two family, cost $7300 on W. 107th off Detroit. The street is fairly well kept. The other homes are nice…Across the street is this large, dirty field, weedy, with train tracks used by the factories on that block. You can see Glidden paint factories and all. I think paint factories are unhealthy, aren't they?

Mom tells me dad would like us to live with them. They are going to take the lower five rooms. (There is an upstairs too.) They really haven't any furniture to put in it. And if we went in with them that would be solved.

But I'm not going in with them. Always telling me to do [things] their way, etc., with the children and all. Of course, they can't help themselves, but I am 28 and can make a few good decisions myself. If I do wrong I can blame only myself. Of course, then I could go out and work and be able to salt some of it away. Lord knows we'll need money when you are home again. But maybe we can manage without the money. We never had too much and managed. I want to have a home of our own from the very minute you get back even if it is only three rooms on Central Avenue. What do you think?

Darling, these last few days I have missed you more than ever. Today was the worst of all. I just can't bear to see a man and wife together with children the age of ours. I'm not jealous, I'm sure of that, it is just that it hurts me. The girls are getting so cute now and that hurts too. You can't be here to see how cute they are. I hope things end soon, dear! It gets so hard to be alone so much. I love you so, hon. I miss you, hon. God watch over you and bring you home safe to me. Soon, very soon.

—Love, Irma, Lola & Di

Chapter 6

1945, Spring: When Will It All End?

April 5 (V-Mail)

Dearest Lou: How are you? There is much fighting going on there. I'm pretty sure you must be in the midst of it. I wasn't prepared this time for the Bull going out. I only received six letters in all this period. It seems you could have written more. In the last [letters] there was a check in each. Of course, you may have written some that can't be passed [by censors] until you are back again. Or maybe you didn't just bother writing. Which is it? Goodnight darling, wherever you are. May God watch over you.

—Love, Irma

Because Irma was living in a neighborhood outside the supportive Hungarian community she had grown up in, she didn't handle change well so she lacked the confidence to deal effectively with the upheaval caused by Lou's absence. She anxiously awaited letters during Operation Iceberg when Lou and his shipmates were engaged in the battle for Okinawa. She was scared. Because of her mother and father's support, she enjoyed a measure of freedom to catch up on her housework, attend a movie, or join her friends for the Friday Night Club outings. But most nights were filled with worry and doubt. She was very much alone and lonely.

For the 4 million or more home front war wives, the stress of being separated from their husbands was magnified by the challenges of managing household and family responsibilities in the face of shortages and rationing. For most wives, this was the first time they filled the role of head of household, and they did so at younger ages because many were newlyweds. Raised among immigrant families, Irma didn't expect any assistance from community resources, and didn't know how to access them anyway.

A number of studies conducted shortly after the war ended revealed how wartime couples had fared during the war and how they adjusted at the husband's return. A 1945 survey of servicemen's wives in Chicago revealed that loneliness and money were the major issues of war wives. Loneliness could be moderate or extreme depending on whether wives worked or were fulltime mothers. Some wives moved in with their families because the government's allotment check was inadequate to cover household expenses.

Home front wives with children often felt isolated from the normality of couples whose husbands had not been drafted. They missed their family life with their husbands. For Irma, it fanned feelings of being separate and different from the people around her, as couples two-stepped through the neighborhood and continued to build their lives while she suffered emotionally and fell behind financially.

Writing letters proved to be crucial for couples in adjusting to separation for the duration of the war. It also improved re-entry of the husband to family life. Lou and Irma exchanged more than 500 letters between 1943 and 1945, writing almost daily during 1944 and 1945. The letters provided a connection from the home front to the battlefront. As the war dragged on, it became more difficult for them to find fresh topics of conversation. Like other wartime couples they found themselves repeating information or feeling they no longer knew each other. Irma felt it was her wifely duty to keep Lou's spirits up, although Lou could tell she was feeling blue and lonely, so she wasn't fooling him.

April 8

Dearest Husband of Mine: Darling, as Lola and I were standing on Madison [Street] waiting for a streetcar, several cars passed us as they do and we never pay any attention to them, but I just happened to glance into one and I got such a shock. I was shaking for a few moments. And yet there was nothing so unusual in it. These were only ordinary people, just a man driving and his wife beside him. She was leaning over into the back to do something for a child looking out of the window. I can't exactly explain why it affected me so. It just seemed strange for people to be still doing things we used to do so often. Just going for a ride. Somehow, it didn't occur to me that people were still doing those things even though we had to give them up. It seemed wrong for them to be doing it in front of us as if they were gloating. (But of course they didn't even notice us on the corner as they slipped by.) And it was silly of me, the world goes on no matter what happens to one little family. Or another one.

I miss you darling, the girls miss you and we are all waiting for the day when we can all do just little ordinary things together. May that day come soon!!!!!!!!!!

God bless you, dear and bring you home soon to us.

—Love Irma—the girls

April 15

Dearest Lou: I hope by this time you are back at your base, although even today the radio commentator keeps talking about the great battles being fought by the Navy for Okinawa.

Of course, the biggest thing that has hit us this week is the death of President Roosevelt. It came as a great shock to all of us. At first we wondered if things would be confused, but now everything is in apple pie order with Truman taking calmly over.

We were at home when we heard the news at about 4:40 p.m. Thursday. I myself didn't hear until I put the radio on. I'll never forget what a shock it was. I'll always remember the surroundings of that moment. And I'll never forget Lola's pink dress that I was ironing when I first heard.

The radio cancelled all programs until Saturday. We heard only men speaking of him, news, and music commemorating his passing. It was all very solemn and beautiful.

Where were you and what were you doing when you heard the news? And what was your reaction. Darling, have I told you I love you? Oh, yes, I see I have! Well, anyway I can say it again if I want, can't I? I love you, I love you.

And take care of yourself for your—"Little Boss"

April 16 (V-Mail)

Dearest Lou: I went to the Hipp [movie theater] tonight and saw A Tree Grows in Brooklyn.

I read the book some time ago and liked it so. I was curious to see what the movie version would be like. I liked it.

I was most interested in the newsreel of the late President [Roosevelt's] life and his time in Washington. But I really wanted to see the invasion of Okinawa, which came out last Tuesday. They didn't show it at the Hipp. So I went to that Telenews place afterwards and saw it. I always have hopes of seeing your ship, although it is very unlikely and even if I did it would add to my uneasiness. It didn't show very much and as usual very little of the ships. The whole thing was very short considering how large the operation was. But I suppose this was only the first batch and more will come after the Island is more securely in our hands. I hope you are back [to your base] by this time.

—Love, Irma

In their reconnaissance of the southern beaches of Okinawa, the *Bull* suffered ongoing firepower attacks by kamikaze pilots; many ships in their vicinity were hit, with some loss of life. Attacks were sometimes so heavy that the ships would be ordered to "make smoke" to hide their positions from the suicide pilots. It was just as well Irma did not know the beating the *Bull* was experiencing in Okinawa during the battle.

The *Bull's* history report filed with the Department of the Navy in October 1945 states "The phrase 'luck of the Bull' took root during the many air raids to which this vessel was subjected. Performance of her crew during the morale-attacking days wherein twilight seemed automatically to produce suicide attacks was truly 'Bully.'"

April 28 (V-Mail)

Dearest Lou: The radio has been humming all day with bits of news of the ending of the war in Europe. But nothing is positive and no one seems to know for sure. Everyone is anxious and ready to be glad. But somehow I can't feel anyway about it. I have waited so long and been over it so many times in my mind. Of course, it would be good news, but it was too long in coming, wore itself out for me.

—Goodnight darling, Irma

April 29 (V-Mail)

Dearest Lou: Your girls, all three of them, were in a vile mood today. Perhaps it has something to do with this gloomy weather. I don't know. Then too, it would be nice to get a letter from you. It gets tiresome going to the mailbox so many times for nothing. I think I'd even welcome a bill! That's the only thing I do get. Phone bills.

Yes, I know I have to lose weight, but there must be an easier way than running up and down three flights of stairs three or four times a day just for mail. Oh well, perhaps before the week is over I'll get two or three.

Well, goodnight darling. Sleep well…I love you, dear.

—Always, Irma

April 29

Dearest Lou: The fight [at Okinawa] seems to be a nasty one and very fierce. Yet even a grand ship like the Bull couldn't be in a battle for so long without rest and reloading so I wonder why she hasn't come back yet. All sorts of ideas run through my mind. Perhaps the Bull is going to have a new base closer to the coming missions and even now you all are setting up and getting settled at this new base. But I must confess I do have some wild ones [thoughts] now and again in the dark of the night, but they are never with me for long. Somehow, I feel my love for you will bring you back to me.

I make it my business to live within the $100 [allowance] I get, no matter how hard I think it gets at times. I want to learn it thoroughly by the time you get home no matter how little or how much (I hope) you make, there will be no words over money anymore. After all, money means so little when you compare it with happiness.

I need to build more confidence in my cooking. So am trying new recipes and getting more practice, but as yet I can't report anything favorable to you on that. But practice makes perfect they say.

God bless you, dear, and watch over you and bring you home soon, very soon to us. We are waiting.

—Yours forever, Irma

P.S. Kisses and hugs from the girls too.

May 3, South Pacific

Dearest One: I got all your letters when we came back to our base, even all your old letters that you sent late. I sure was glad to get so many at one time, tho it sure was a surprise to me after not getting any letter from you for two whole months. Oh, darling of mine, you're just wonderful to write such sweet letters to me, and so many of them too.

I'm sorry, hon, I couldn't write to you sooner, was busy as hell this time for we were at Okinawa the last few weeks and on top of that was kinda sick, nothing serious, tho, just a good cold (sore throat) with a high temperature. So was laid up for a few days before going back to base, not the same one this time. I think we are going to have a new base from now on. It's not the one you wrote about in your last letter, but it is pretty close to that place. It really is nice over here, the sun is always shining with blue skies all around, hardly ever rains here but I suppose when it does, it pours. It really is a lot hotter here than at the other place, but at least it's better to sweat away then to be catching colds like we were, it was always so damp at night and cold.

I suppose the weather will be changing here for summer is starting, so I guess it won't be so bad now. [Remainder of letter missing]

May 6, North Pacific

Dearest Little Wife of Mine: I received your letter of April 8. I am so very lonely and blue for you too. I understand how it is with you, dear, you have it much harder than me, because you see other couples together with their children and oh so many things going on that we were doing when we were together, if only I could do something about it and make you happy again. But that's just the trouble, I can't do anything for you except to say that I love you very much, so much so that it hurts me so to know that I can't be near you.

Will close now, dear, it is getting late, am going on watch at midnight till four in the morning. So, good night, my love, until tomorrow.

—love to you always

May 8, North Pacific

Dearest, Wife of mine: It is still raining here, coming down pretty hard. We are finally leaving this place and damn glad of it for there are still some kamikaze planes coming around. Going back to our new base again, it sure will be good to get some of that sunshine even if I start sweating all over, at least it's better than being in the damp weather. Furthermore, it always feels good to set one's feet on dry land even just for a while.

Glad to hear you are still seeing and going to the [neighbor's apartment], at least you have some place to go to even if you have to help her with her dresses. Her husband always was a good scout in helping out anyone. I'm sure glad he helped you home with Lola through all that ice and snow.

—Love Forever. Love to kids too.

May 11, South Pacific

Dearest One: Darling, from what I hear about Lola she must be a big girl now, bless her little heart, if only I could see her now, in fact all of you. Maybe I will sometime this year, will let you know more about it when I know for sure. Anyway, I'm sure it will be this summer, always thinking of what we will do, where we will go, and oh so many things.

So if it doesn't come about, will see all of you for good next year around this time for we finally heard that the war is over in Europe, I sure am glad it is over with over there.

No doubt now Johnny [his brother] will be home for good, I hope. Because some of them [soldiers] will be sent over here to get it [the war] over with as quick as possible, it can't get over quick enough for me.

I keep wondering how it will feel to be home again knowing that I wouldn't have to leave you my dear, for I'm so tired of all this killing of one another and I know that you are too. Tired of always being alone, always going by yourself, whenever you go out seeing other young couples together. I know just how you feel, dear, so with God's help all this will be over with soon.

So, Good Night my sweet, you are always in my mind, your name on my lips as I go to bed each night.

—Forever, Lou

May 20

Dear Lou: Friday May 11 the club went out to the Alpine Village to celebrate some new pregnant mothers. I had a swell, swell time! You were there with me every moment! We sat opposite the little table we had the night we went there together. To make it more perfect, at our little table [from our dinner there] sat a serviceman and his woman (wife or sweetheart). He was an Army man, but all night I kept referring to him as "the sailor." The girls thought I was wacky.

Oh, my dear, darling, when you come home the first night we shall have to go and have at least one Manhattan at the Alpine. You and I at our little table. Shall we?

Darling, I love you, I love you, I love you, I love you.

—Your "Little Boss"

P.S. The girls send love and kisses.

May 26, South Pacific

Dearest Irma: I haven't heard from you for a couple days now, hope there isn't anything wrong at home? Or anybody else? I was hoping I would hear from you today, but there wasn't any letters from anybody. I'm still hoping, for there is still tomorrow, our last day here. Maybe if I don't get any here, I'll get some of your letters at the next place we stop.

It sure feels like hell when I don't hear from you. Now I know how you must feel when you don't hear from me. When I do start getting your letters, I hope there won't be too many V-mails among them.

Yesterday, I sent home some pictures that were taken out here, 23 all together. So let me know if you get them. I want to share them with my grandchildren, and my children too, some day when they grow up. So put all of them in my Navy book.

My darling, I miss you so, every time I see a movie with a dark-haired woman in it, I don't really see her at all. I see you instead of her. Do you know what I mean, dearest? I'm sure you do because we love one another so much that you and I can see those little things. Oh, my darling, I love you so much, so much that it hurts inside of me knowing that we are so far apart from each other. But some day soon, we will be together again.

—Love always, Lou

May 29, South Pacific

My Dearest One: We left today with a slow convoy, it will take some time before we get where we're going, can't tell you the place we're going to. Also, it will be some time before you get this letter, and there will be bunches of them, for I hope to write at least one page a day, so you won't be so lonely and blue from not hearing from me.

We were at our base for 15 days and in all that time I only got two letters from you. But they really weren't letters at all for one of them was a father's day's card and the other one was your picture, so you see I didn't really hear from you as much as I was hoping I would. Then I heard they had sent our letters and packages to our old base or to the place we are going to now, so maybe I'll get some letters yet. Gee, I hope so for it really gets me down not hearing from you and keeps me worrying about whether you're all right at home. I hope to God you all are in good health.

—Lou

Erratic mail delivery was a fact of war and took a toll on servicemen and their wives, playing havoc with their emotions on both the home front and battlefront. The *Bull's* log book for 1945 recounts their role as "mailmen," transferring mailbags to other APDs and carriers. Packages and letters easily went astray as servicemen changed locations.

One war wife cleverly created a newsletter for her husband, a paratrooper in the Army stationed in the European theater. "The Goofein Journal" was hand-lettered on card stock and full of news and drawings about family events and friends. Marion Reh Gurfein's story is one of the few stories by a home front wife captured in the Library of Congress Veterans History Project database.

Marion penned a humorous poem to express her frustration at being cut off for long periods of time from her husband's letters.

Goofy Gremlins

A Gremlin cross the ocean
Had a gay and impish notion
And said, "how about our holding back
The Goofy Gurfein's mail?"

The Gremlins all were willing
For they found the idea thrilling
So they kept the letters locked away
Until the news was stale.

Then they sent it out in snatches
And in great unwieldy batches,

With the postmarks all a hodge-podge
And the mailman turning gray.

And although things now are humming
And the letters keep on coming.
There are STILL some letters hidden
Up until this very day!!!

—Marion Reh Gurfein, 1940s

May 31, South Pacific

My Dearest Wife: We are still at sea, still going slow as ever for the other ships can't go any faster, so we have to drag along with them, but I don't mind going this slow for a change. For one thing, at least we don't get any spray. It's rather calm ever since we left our base. And I'm glad for once we don't take any spray for when my clothes get wet from this damn salt water, they get stiff as a board and make one's body itch. Even now I'm taking saltwater showers, but after all it's better than nothing at all.

Darling, it's such a pretty sight when one goes out to sea. At night you can see the sun go down, it seems to go right into the water, and later on I see the moon come right out, and the clouds. It really is a pretty sight to see.

Also, to see these flying fish come out right in front of the ship, they fly about 50 yards ahead, then dive into the water, then all over again they do the same thing, while others go different ways. Many was the time I found some on deck and threw them overboard, for when the sea is rough and the wind is strong they fly right up on our ship. They are a pretty blue like the sea. They are about eighteen inches long. This is all I could think of to write tonight, maybe tomorrow will be better.

—Love, Lou

June 4

Darling "Big Boss:" I am sorry you haven't been getting any letters. I can't understand it. There are some you haven't gotten that you should have by this time, not mentioning the Christmas packages which are likely lost. It makes me pretty sad and sore too to have those things lost. Have you been getting the letters with the [Cleveland Plain Dealer] "Home Front Press" [column]? No wonder I never get any answers to my questions.

Darling, tonight I bought that black nightgown that is your birthday gift to me. Boy, it sure is nice. It is all black, form fitting! It has three small bouquets of forget-me-nots embroidered along the front of it, so you'd better hurry home!

Lola Lee keeps calling you every day "Come, come, come home Daddy," beckoning with her little hands. And I guess she puts my thoughts into words.

—Goodnight my dear, Irma

P.S. Gown cost $5.00

June 5

[Greeting and first paragraph missing]

Bank (funds)	*$231.02*
$50.00 Bonds	*112.50*
$25.00 Bonds	*75.00*
	$418.52

Not bad, hon, is it. Maybe we can buy a little house after all when you get back, adding your discharge money with it. It doesn't have to be an expensive home. Just something we can carry with ease. Then after that is paid for we can always buy a better one. By that time the girls would be old enough to appreciate it. Well,

we can toy with the idea until you get home. Then we shall see. What say you?

I still wear my hair as when I was in New York only I have fatter rolls [of hair] and it comes high on my head. Looks pretty neat. Although I still have a lot of trouble with my hair.

Love to you, darling. I'll write you some night when I can really write in ease and whisper sweet nothings in your ear.

—Your "Little Boss, " Irma & the girls

On June 4 while leaving Saipan to return to Okinawa from a maintenance check on the *Bull*, the *Bull's* convoy encountered a horrific typhoon with wildly violent winds and mountainous seas. The wind blew at 70 knots (81 mph). The convoy reversed course, hoping to avoid the typhoon, but they were unable to escape it. When a typhoon raged, the crew could only move about on the deck by hanging onto the steel cables along the perimeter. They might be strapped into their bunks, and hot meals were not available. Luckily, none of the ships or their crews in the convoy suffered casualties. Lou never talked much about his tour of duty in the Pacific Theater in the fight for Iwo Jima and Okinawa, but the force of the typhoon stuck with him forever.

"We hit such strong winds, the ship rode up one side of these high waves and hesitated for a minute before it plunged back into the ocean," he said. "The waves were as tall as a building. I worried that it wouldn't ride the wave back down, but turn over instead." The typhoon was so powerful that it damaged some of the plates on the *Bull's* hull.

The *Bull* made a third and final voyage to Okinawa on June 8 and remained until July 1 when it departed and steamed with its task force to San Pedro, California, for repairs, training, and to host UDT rehearsals for the invasion of Japan.

June 5, South Pacific

Dearest Irma: I am writing this letter on the 6th of June for yesterday I didn't have time to write for we were fighting a typhoon. It was a fierce one, and last one, I hope. Boy, we rolled around just like a cork in water. The only time I got scared was when the ship would roll over to one side and then back to the other side. It just seemed to hang there for a second then would right itself and shudder just like she herself was afraid. But she took it like a fighting ship should. There was a strong wind blowing—100 miles or more an hour, and waves high as 70 to 90 feet, it was even coming over our fantail, knocking everything around and over the side. I don't think any man would have had a chance if he was washed over the side for those waves would either pull him down under or smash him to bits against the hull, even Old Glory was torn to shreds by the wind.

I hope I never have to go through that again, once is enough. I would sooner see a dozen Japanese planes coming at us, at least you can fight them off. But not a typhoon, we can't very well fight that off, just ride it out and pray. Love to all.

—Love, Lou

June 6, South Pacific

My Darling Wife: As I told you in my other letter about the typhoon, it sure was hell while it lasted. Before it started the sea was calm, smooth as glass, not even a breeze in the air as we started to run for it. We tried to get out of the way but I guess it was too wide to escape. To really picture it one must be in it and see it with one's own eyes.

So anyway, it hit us early in the morning, lasted about six hours while I was sleeping below, slept through the worst of it. I had to laugh at some of the fellows for they had two life jackets on, one that goes around your waist while another one is a Mae West life preserver [named after the buxom movie star]. They were so darn scared that they couldn't even talk, even shaking like jelly as they were standing around topside, for not one of them would stay below decks. What a mess it was afterwards, water all over the ship, so we had plenty of work to do today. My compartment was a mess also, water here and there which made the decks like ice, had to hang on to things walking around down here.

—Love to all, my Love, Lou

June 13, South Pacific, at Sea

Dearest One: You ask me in your V-Mail whether I'm fed up with this roaming around or not. Well, I sure am fed up. When I get out of this Navy I never want to see another ocean as long as I live or another Navy ship. It's really hell being away from you and the children. All I see out here is water and blue skies and other ships, also the islands, which I can't even set my feet on. Now and then a little action—I think if it weren't for these little fights and your sweet letters now and then, I'd go nuts out here. But we always find something to do. When I am through with my cleaning up I usually sit down on my locker and write to you as I'm doing now.

It's a little too warm for me up in the mess hall so I stay down here by my bunk sitting on my locker with a blower blowing cool air at me.

So you want to know if I would like to come out here again after the war is over? I would like that very much if you were with me, that would be more like it. After all, I can't enjoy all these pretty sights by myself. It would be nice if we could afford to come out here for another honeymoon. I'm all for it as there are plenty of nice islands around here, and all the sunshine one wants.

—Love Always, Lou

June 16, South Pacific, at Sea

Dearest Irma: In several of your letters you ask how we felt when we heard the war was over in Europe, also about the President's death.

Well, about the President's death, when I heard about it we were out on patrol and when one of the fellows told us about it, we didn't believe him. We were kinda surprised, some of us wondered what would happen now. So then we started to talk about our vice president taking over to finish the job, we are sure he will pull us through in everything.

Now, about the war being over, we were glad to hear of it. We kinda expected it to be over soon, we all were happy to hear it, for now we will get more help out here and get this one [Pacific War] over with as soon as possible, the quicker the better. Know what, darling, just between you and me, I think this war will be over with all of a sudden.

So, you have sent me three more packages, you're a darling little wife, you make me love you all the more. Did I tell you how much I love your cakes and cookies, you sure know how to make them so that they just melt in one's mouth. I sure miss them, dear. It's too bad it takes so much time for them to get here. Thank your mother for me and the girls for making those cookies for me. Will be thinking of all of you every bite I take.

Today was payday. Will not send any money home this time, for I need a new pair of shoes, will wait until next pay, then will send all the money home.

—Loving you always, Lou

June 18, South Pacific, at sea

Dearest Little Boss: The two letters I got today are dated June 4 and 7. It seems we are now getting better mail service. Yes, I always get the home front press column in your letters and all those clippings you have sent. The one about those sailors and their beards is pretty good. I haven't got my beard anymore, but I have a handlebar mustache, looks pretty good on me (ha-ha). It comes to a point at the ends and upward.

Say, honey, is that all your going to get for your birthday, that gown was pretty cheap. I thought it would be more than that. Get something else, or do you want to wait until I get home or maybe I'll be able to buy something out here that would remind us of the years we were apart?

I am sleepy now, so will close with love.

—Love, Lou

June 19

Dearest Lou: Harry [Lou's brother-in-law] called me to let me know that Margaret got a telegram from [your brother] Johnny. They expect him home sometime tomorrow night. We have all been waiting such a long, long time!

Harry gave a surprise house-warming party for Margaret last Saturday. The party was swell. To be honest I was a little hesitant of going, but couldn't say no because of hurting all of them.

There were about twelve of us, eight couples and three war wives. We gave Margaret $5.00 in a nice card, and also contributed a bottle of liquor and two boxes of my cookies. (I got a lot of compliments on my cookies, ahem.)

[One of the husbands] said he thought my cookies were very good, no wonder you wanted to come home. So I said, "Oh, no! That isn't why he wants to come home." They all thought the remark was pretty funny. Well, it may have been, but darn it, the situation isn't a bit humorous is it?

Being [at the party] shows just how lonely a woman can be without her man around.

I hope you are getting my letters regularly by this time. If only you could be here with us at home.

I'm so lonely—Irma

July 5, South Pacific, at base

Dearest Irma: We got here early this morning. This is the first time we have been at this base. We may be here for a couple of days. Boy, it seems twice as hot here then back at our regular base. We are now anchored in the bay, it really looks nice here too with long rolling hills and palm trees swaying in the breeze. I would like to set my feet on this island, then I can say that I have been on it, might as well for I have just about been on all these islands out here. It really looks pretty from here for we are close to the beach. It is fixed up nice with a ball field on one side and tables and benches to sit and drink. On top of the hill you can see the Red Cross canteen. It seems no matter where we go we always see a Red Cross canteen. They are ok, everything is free, doughnuts, coffee, ice tea, but no milk. I would like some milk for a change. The next chance I get, I'm going to drink plenty of it.

I received your letter today. It made me happy when I read about everything, especially about Johnny being discharged. If only I could do the same, calling on the telephone to say I am coming home for good. Darling, I don't think that day is far off now. Yes, dear, I guess it takes a while before one does get discharged for there are so many of us.

I also get a funny feeling in my tummy when I think about me coming home and how I will act when I see you and the children. I love you so, dear, and will write more. It is very late now, taps have already sounded.

—Goodnight, my love, Lou

July 13

Dearest Lou: We are all well now. I was sick for a couple days over the weekend, but it was nothing serious.

When the girls were over for club at my house, I took my new black nightgown out to show them. They all kidded me about how

handy I have it, right there in the hall chest. They said I'm ready for you to walk in the door and out will come my black gown. It seems like all the other service wives have their gowns packed away in mothballs.

Well, mom had given me some money. I spent some for a new girdle, but still had some of it left. I did think I needed some new slack sets and play clothes. I bought material for a royal blue pair [of slacks], and material for a 3-piece playsuit set in aqua with black stripes, although I should be sewing for my mom and the kids. I haven't even started my house cleaning and it's almost fall and I should start the fall sewing. What's the matter with me?

So long for now, dear! Here's a big kiss from me to you (X) and from Lola Lee (X), and don't forget Diane (X).

—Love, Irma

July 17

Dearest: Sometimes I miss you so, dear. I just think I can't go on for another day. I go to bed and honestly don't care if I ever wake up again. It gets just too, too hard to go on alone like this. But then I look at the girls and scrape up enough energy to go on again after all, they are part of my duties. Surely, if you can do your part so valiantly, I should be able to do my part bravely. Your part is so much more disheartening than mine.

Just how and what to do until you get home. To have everything all set for when you do get home [on leave]. To have all the time free that I can when you are home with us. I resolve to do everything too. But then I begin to feel sad and everything goes haywire.

I just can't do anything without great effort and some things never get done. When I feel blue and lonesome I don't want to do anything, I just want to think of you.

I'm glad you feel you will want me near you always when you are home for I have been wondering about that. For I know I'm

going to make a pest of myself and never let you out of my sight. Oh, my darling, my dear darling. I love you!

Love-Love-Love-Irma

July 23

Darling Lou: I received another letter from you this morning dated July 16. There was a small part of the first sheet cut out [by the censors], also most of the last sheet was gone. However, I am more and more convinced you are now at Guam. What I can't figure out is the purpose of your trip. I am very, very glad you are away from all the fighting around Japan. At least I hope you are. I can never be sure anyway.

Somehow I just can't get rid of the idea that I'll see you before the summer is over. Silly, aren't I? My mind tells me I'm so darn silly, but my heart tells me to keep on hoping. You know my heart always rules my mind. I think now, looking back, I bought the material for those sports clothes with that in the back of my mind. Aren't I the foolish one? Boy, will I be the disappointed one when summer passes and you aren't home.

Irma-Lola Lee-Diane

August 1, San Pedro, California

Dearest Wife of Mine: So you want to know just where I am in California. We are in San Pedro now in dry dock at Todd's Shipyard, but we may pull out of here today and go to the Navy yard and stay until the first group on leave comes back.

Then the second group will go on their leave and then I guess the rest of us will go out to sea close by for more training. Yes, will train in cold water for its pretty cold where we are going when we get back to the Japanese again. But I hope, dear, that it is over with by the time we are ready to leave.

Darling, I'm so glad you think I write mushy letters to you, that's the way I always try to write my letters, for that's the way I feel about you. I think I can express my words and feelings better in person when I am with you. I love you.

—Love to all, Lou

August 1

Dearest Lou: I received your letter of July 29, no need to say how disappointed I am and we all are that you are only getting seven days [leave]. I was planning on thirty. I guess I should be glad you are coming home at all.

Well, we will crowd thirty days into seven, won't we? Just so we can be together, even for a little while. Funny, before you call each night I sit and look out the window with lights out and think of you and I think if only I could just be with him for an hour or half-hour or even five minutes. Just to see him and touch him and hear him say personally he's "all right."

Now I'm going to have you for seven days and I'm still complaining! Us women, we are never satisfied!

—Love to you, Darling

August 13

Dearest Lou: I have already taken out your white summer robe and slippers. Also, dad brought over the case of beer I asked him to get me. I also have two bottles of the best liquor and a bottle of very good rum. The new period of rationing starts on the 18th, so then I'll get more. Anyway, I don't think we will have to worry about that after V-J [Victory over Japan] day is here.

Isn't it wonderful, darling, how everything turned out? I am hoping you won't have to go out again, but if you do, dear, I'll be patient and be thankful that you won't be in danger anyway, fighting. But I do hope you can stay with me for good.

Darling, we have so much to bind us together, I just know we will always be happy together, just like the endings in the fairy tales, you know, "and they lived happily ever after."

After all this trouble and unhappiness, we will spend our lives just wonderful. Like a fine play. The stage is set. The actors are all in their places, just waiting for the curtain to raise and the hero to enter. Life for us shall be forever after just a wonderful drama!!! Love drama, mostly.

—Love, Irma, X

For some reason Lou never made it home on leave when stationed in California for ship repairs. To have him back in the country and not be able to see him overwhelmed Irma. She suffered bouts of depression. Her patience and patriotism as a dutiful war wife were tested. And yet, she saw the gold stars honoring the death of husbands and sons hanging in the windows of houses on the street and was relieved they had escaped that fate.

Lou's niece Jeanne wrote him when the war ended in Europe.

"Uncle Louis," she said, "since Germany surrendered, things are much better. There is no longer a midnight curfew for shows and nightclubs. The brownout, which required all windows, show lights and other lights to be darkened is over! I am so happy, and now just need to have you home."

When Johnny came home at the end of June after serving in Europe and Africa the family had a celebration. Johnny wrote to Lou, "I am so glad to be home. You should be glad that you are not in the Army, at least you have a bed to sleep in, not a foxhole. And can take a bath or shower, not by using a helmet full of water." This was of little consolation to Lou. His ship was scheduled to participate in the invasion of Japan.

Chapter 7

1945, Fall: The Home Stretch

Irma was giddy with excitement. The war in the Pacific had ended. She had a small celebration with her parents over what she hoped would be Lou's speedy homecoming. "How long will that take?" she said. "It can't come soon enough for me. It truly will be a Merry Christmas again."

The Japanese surrendered on August 15, 1945, which became known as Victory over Japan (V-J) day. The surrender papers were officially signed on September 2. The long journey home for enlisted personnel followed a demobilization plan using a complicated point system. But no matter, the war was finally over! Husbands, fathers, sons, and brothers would return home; shortages and rationing would end; scarce items like tires, shoes, and cotton fabrics would be available once again; new steel appliances would be on the market again. The war was over!

In New York City, millions gathered in Times Square on August 14, waiting for the official announcement. People from all walks of life filled the streets. When the surrender was finally announced, the excited crowd roared, grabbed their loved ones, and hugged and kissed each other. The immediacy of the moment was captured forever when sailor George Mendonsa embraced nurse Greta Z. Friedman (she was really a dental assistant) for a heartfelt kiss. The scene was snapped for posterity by photojournalist Alfred

Eisenstaedt, *Life* magazine's renowned war photographer. It was *Life's* leading image in its V-J spread in the August 27, 1945, issue.

Other servicemen who were milling around in Times Square also remembered the event. "On August 14, 1945, I was in New York headed for Times Square," said a sailor from the Merchant Marine, "where there was a Pepsi-Cola canteen: Hot dogs were a nickel, and Pepsis were free. I saw this sailor grab a nurse and kiss her. Of course, I had seen that more than once on the square. But in front of the couple were two photographers snapping away. Just as that was happening, it came around on the news ticker on the side of the building: The war is over! The war is over!"

Another New Yorker went to Times Square in Manhattan with her brother and his girlfriend. "It was New Year's Eve all over again," she said. "Several military personnel attempted to kiss me. I was eager to do my part for the military, but she [my sister-in-law] blocked every attempt at a kiss! I joke today that I might have been on the cover of *Life* if not for her!"

Not to be outdone by New Yorkers, Clevelanders partied in the downtown streets as well, leaving them strewn with streamers. Not discouraged by heavy rain, residents drove through the streets beeping car horns, ringing cowbells, and blowing whistles. Servicemen kissed their wives and girlfriends. Smaller neighborhood celebrations were just as enthusiastic with toilet paper streamers thrown from second-story windows and hugging and kissing of friends and family.

Irma's brother Chuck wrote to her about how the announcement was received by his fellow Navy crew members at sea: "Sis, visualize if you can the crew after a blistering, suffocating day, having showered, sitting around a table, some writing, some playing cards, and still others just sitting idly. Suddenly, the music the men had been listlessly listening to was abruptly stopped, and the paralyzing news issued: the Japanese government was willing to accept the peace offer consummately. I cannot describe the tumult, the generally gleeful crew were literally wild with gladness. A celebration of no small means ensued, with a few still tenaciously clinging to the radio for further information or confirmation of the announcement."

When Japan surrendered, the *Bull* was still undergoing repairs in California. It was soon reassigned to assist in cleanup efforts in the Philippines, transporting troops and supplies for occupation forces and ferrying decommissioned servicemen to homeward-bound ships. For Lou and Irma, the pain of separation was almost too much to bear any longer, and their letters spilled over with their frustrations with the demobilization process, and declarations of love and longing.

August 21

Dear Lou: Darling, oh my darling, I'm such a fool. I should have waited for official news of how many points you have. This way I had you home with me already and now it shall be unbearable to go on alone as usual for the remaining few months. I know I should be thankful that the war is over (and I am) and be content just knowing you will be safe, but I just want you home.

I'm always complaining, aren't I? Only a few more, isn't it? But honestly, hon, I just can't help myself, I'm just crazy with loneliness for you. I want you home with us. I want a normal life for us again as before this hellish nightmare.

I love you, I love you—Irma

August 31

Dearest Lou: I got your letter of the 28th yesterday and felt a little hope return. Maybe, just maybe, we may see each other soon. Oh dear, I hope so!

Yes, I think I remember where you said you'd go on the phone [when we talked]. But what matters more is whether you are coming back into the states or going out.

The girls are both talking about "daddy." Lola Lee keeps building trains out of her blocks because her daddy is coming home. Each train or train tracks we pass are the ones you are coming on. Every once in awhile Lola Lee is looking out the window and sees a sailor suit, mostly the white ones, and insists that "that's daddy coming."

I did go out with a friend Wednesday evening to a show and coffee to drown my sorrows. It helped, but still it will be sometime before I can get used to the idea that I won't see you after all in the immediate future [because the Navy canceled your leave].

Darling, I get so fed up with everything and yet I shouldn't be. I have it so much better than most service wives.

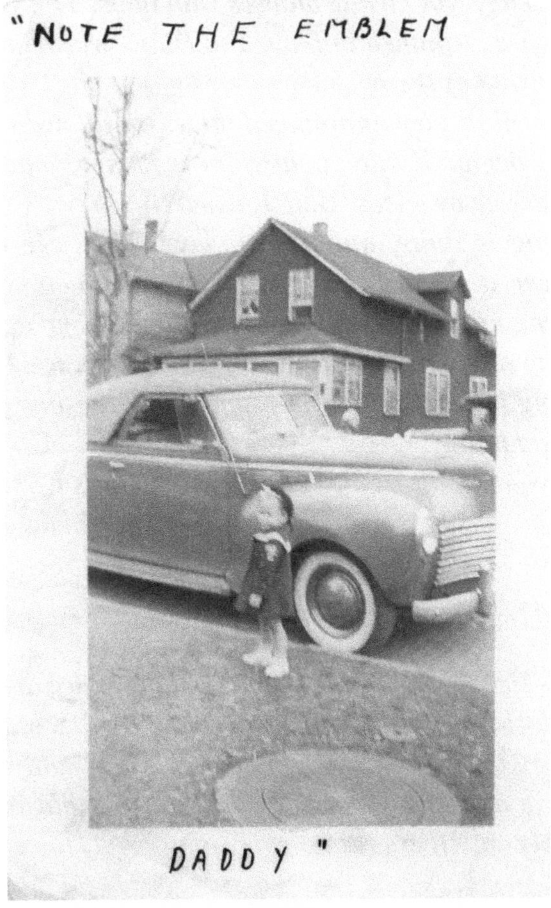

Dear, the girls are the cutest girls in the world! They jibber-jabber all day, both of them

We all love you and sure would like to be with you, but what to do about it? Just wait and wait and wait!

—Love to you, my dearest darling, Irma & the girls

September 10

Dear Lou: Yesterday was the Hungarian Festival at the hall on 41st [Street] where it is always held. Mom, dad, the girls and I went. It was the same as usual except for the shortage of men.

The girls looked so cute, I made them each a blouse and jumper set. They wore white blouses with them. The set belonging to Lola Lee was trimmed in blue, and Diane was trimmed in red. I felt very proud of them.

This morning they announced the extra allowances they are making [for demobilization points] for the Navy, ¼ point for each month of service overseas. Generous, aren't they.

The gang is quite, quite these days. They are almost over drinking beer, it's fancy cocktails even for the men. So you better start catching up and become modern, but ultra! Of course, where we are going to get the money is something else. It does look as if we are going to be the "poor relations" for reasons you will see when you get home.

I hope you are all right. Let me know what's what.

—Love, Irma & the girls

September 12, at sea

Dearest One: Today is the sixth day that we are at sea. We will get to Pearl Harbor today around 1600 hours. We may stay there for a couple days, then we might come back. I really don't know now what we may do. There is a swell chance that we will come back soon because there are so many of us ready to be discharged.

There are about 50 fellows to be discharged all together, but I am sorry to say I am not among these 50 for I only have 41¾ points now that they have changed the point system around. Don't be blue now, baby, I'm still sure I'll be home for good this year. If not this year then the first of January for sure, because then I'll have 44 points on the head. Also there is a chance they will change the point system around again. They might even lower the points next time. As of this month I have 19 months of sea duty which is not enough to get out now. I'll be counting my points.

Well, here we are ahead of time, can see land already. We are about 50 miles from land, but will be having some gun firing today, even now we are maneuvering around just like when we hit the Japanese. There are seven of us [ships], all APDs. And all of us have new boots aboard, just young kids, most of them. You should have seen these poor kids the first time that they were out to sea, all were pretty sick. They looked pretty funny, running back and forth from the head [bathroom] and to the rail of the ship. They were lined up just like they were watching a game or something and heaving their heads off, they were a sick lot for awhile. But now they are over it and act kind of salty. But they sure have a long way to go before they can call themselves salty.

Well, dear, now that they don't censor our letters anymore, I can write you a lot more things that I couldn't write about before.

There are signs all over the ship asking if anyone cares to ship over to the regular Navy now, and he will be given 30 to 60 days leave and $250 to boot. So what do you say to this, should I sign up or not? (Ha! Ha!) Man, they couldn't keep me in this outfit for all the money in the world. For I love my three little girls more than anything and want to be with them the rest of my life. I love you. I love you.

—Love to my three girls, Lou

Soon after the Japanese surrendered, America's armed services announced plans for the demobilization of 7.5 million men and women. The Navy would discharge 327,000 sailors by October 15, with the remainder of sailors scheduled for discharge over the following 18 months. A point system for release was instituted in September 1945: 44 points were required for enlisted men; 49 points were required for officers.

To be considered for discharge or separation, Lou needed to prove that he had amassed a minimum of 44 points or credits using a complicated formula established by the Navy. The points were calculated from the day he was available for active duty in 1943 and included credit for age, length of service, overseas duty, and number of dependents at home. The total was changed several times over the fall. On November 1, the required number of points was dropped to 39, and Lou was able to show that he had 43.25 points in accordance with the amended demobilization plan. His commanding officer signed off on his report and Lou was in line for a ride home on a fellow APD to a U.S. receiving station. It would prove to be a long wait, as it was for other unhappy servicemen trying to get home after V-J day; the war was over, but they were still on duty. It stretched into a three-month ordeal as the Navy attempted to downsize and return to peacetime conditions.

While Irma waited anxiously, impatiently, Lou suffered bouts of boredom and loneliness sailing to and fro across the South Pacific Ocean to bus other returning servicemen home.

September 16-17, Pearl Harbor

Dearest Irma: Well, dear, we're leaving for Guam on the 19th, maybe. They might change our orders again, you can't tell, hon, this Navy works funny as hell. All the other ships left a couple days ago. The reason we didn't go is because we have to go in dry dock and have the hull of the ship welded where she split apart from the typhoon we went through. Coming over here, it happened again, split apart more, so we were taking in water up forward. Some of the officers were afraid we would sink out there, but we got here without any trouble, had the pumps working all the way.

Darling, I'm sorry to hear you're having money trouble, so maybe this $80.00 will help you out for a while. I don't need it out here. I should have sent it home to you when we were in the states but I was hoping that I would still get my leave. I only wish I could send you more.

—Goodnight, my love, love to my girls, Lou

September 21

Dearest Lou: I got your letter with the $80.00 yesterday. Thank you dear, I think I may spend some of it, although I shouldn't. We'll need it more when you get home.

You ask about the rest of money in the bank. Let me see, there was $231.00 at its fullest before I sent you $41.00, leaving $190.00. I took out $60.00 to pay a long overdue charge account at the May Co. [department store], so I wouldn't have it to worry about while you were here on furlough. Don't ask me what was on the bill at May's. Mostly clothing and gift articles, I guess. I think they were necessities, but you may not think so when you see the list. But you and I always disagreed on that subject. After that I had to take out $30.00 more because I just didn't have any of my [allowance] check left the month you were to come home and didn't. I had gotten so many extra things I wouldn't have otherwise. Out of the $30.00 I bought myself a pair of shoes, yet there are a million and one things I do need here as I look around so I may spend the $80.00. I'm tired of trying to bleed a turnip. If it has to be gotten or fixed sooner or later, it may as well be. I'll let you know.

—So love from me to you, Irma—I love you

October 1

My Darling Irma: Today was payday for us, not a hell of lot for me, though. Only $22.00 dollars is all I get for two weeks. All together every month I get $44.00 dollars. How well I remember the hard days I used to work for $22.00 dollars a week. At that time, it was pretty troubled all over and $22.00 dollars was big money. I'm going to save all my pay now, so when I do come home we will have something to go out with and have a good time before I (we) settle down to the business of getting a house for us.[Remainder of letter lost]

October 2

Dearest Lou: I'm getting more and more impatient for you to be home. I just can't take it anymore. It seems like I only had enough energy til the war was over and after that, poof! No more. I've just got to have my man back, and that's no kidding!

Well, I am now banking on having you home for Xmas. If that falls through, I don't really think I'll take it well. I just can't bare to think of you missing Xmas with us this year. The girls are both of an age where they will enjoy it fully. Lola Lee is talking about Santa Claus, and trees and toys. Oh, my dearest, it would be such a wonderful holiday if only you could be with us to enjoy it!

Enclosure—Irma sent a newspaper ad from *The Cleveland Plain Dealer* for the new 1946 Oldsmobile car with the comment, "Our next car, Ha-Ha!"

—Love, Irma

"Where is the war wife who only the other day was worrying about her own family problems of post-war adjustment? Who grew blue and despondent just thinking about the job ahead of her when her man would come home and once more would have to get acquainted with his wife and children, to assume the responsibility of getting a job and settling down?"

Irma mailed a newspaper clipping of the column, "All's Rosy Now in the Service Wife's World," from *The Cleveland Plain Dealer's* September 1945 edition to Lou because it reflected her concerns and those of other war wives at the time. "That woman who was getting so much conflicting advice on how to treat her returned serviceman. Where is that harassed and lonely creature?"

According to this columnist, whose earlier columns during the war had advised women about the problems of post-war adjustments, "There is just one thing on her mind now. When is Joe coming home? How many days, how many weeks, how many months?

"And, oh yes, she has another problem or two. But she'll solve them. They're really simple—though they seem stupendous at the moment. What is she going to wear when she meets her man at the railroad station.

"There may be tough problems ahead of her—and later she may need advice—but not now. Not on anything more serious than, say, is her new permanent really becoming.

That 'poor little war wife' is the happiest woman in the world."

Their men would soon be home! Irma and the millions of other home front wives were waiting, unhappily, thankfully, to be reunited with their husbands. They were ready to return to a normal life with their husbands by their side to share the life they had lived before the war started.

October 6, Guam

My Darling: I hope there isn't anything wrong with you at home, the reason I say this is that I haven't received any letters from you for a couple days now. I only have gotten one letter from you since we have been here.

We left [Pearl Harbor] on the 21st, got here 2nd of October, we just took our time coming over here. We had movies on the fantail every night. It seemed funny sailing along with the lights on after going around with no lights on at all for so long. It really is a swell feeling knowing that the war is over and we can smoke topside now. Not like before when we had to watch out for subs and planes day and night. Now it's nice and peaceful out here and one can see plenty of sharks.

Well, dear, we still don't know whether we are going to Manila or not. Instead, I hope we come right back home. So here's all my love to my three sweet girls of mine. I love you, hon.

XXX XXX XXX.
—Short timer, Lou

October 9

Dearest Lou: I received a letter from you today and now I feel better...if only you are really coming back to the states as you think you might, and...you are right about your other guesses. If! If! If! Well, it won't be long now, one way or the other.

The girls wait for Lou to come home. (1945)

I have it all figured out about how long it would take you boys to get home once you do reach the Toledo [Ohio] discharge center. It does seem close, doesn't it?

My Aunt Agnes in New York has received word from her adopted daughter in Europe. She went through some pretty terrifying experiences alone. She is now in Slovakia, which is far from her own little village in Romania. She last saw her village in 1942 and even then every man in it was in the army, all my uncles, even the one near 50 [years of age]. One of my nephews has died and several were reported missing.

I feel so ashamed when I think how I've been complaining and feeling blue because of my little part in this war. Just thinking of them makes me feel like I've been living very well indeed compared to those in Europe.

We're lucky, darling, you and I. Lucky in everything, considering. Can't wait to see you again. It will be like a dream.

—Love, Irma-Lola Lee-Diane

October 11, Guam

Darling, Irma: Well, dear, still haven't heard anything from you yet, hoping there isn't anything wrong with you or the girls. I know you are writing to me so somehow my mail must be held up somewhere. I'm not the only one that hasn't received any mail, so doggone it I should get one today.

I'm always so afraid when I don't hear from you that something may of happened to you. Nothing must happen to you, dear, please see to that.

I'll be home soon, darling, you'll see, for they have just cut the points down to 39 on the first of November. You probably know about it, don't you? So I'm hoping we don't go out too far because I'm sure of coming home this year.

Darling, they have changed our orders like I said they would. We are going to Leyte Island, taking ten officers and 100 enlisted men. It will take about three or four days to get there. Leyte is this side of the Philippines.

I hope that's the farthest we go. I am so sick of this roaming around, it's such a waste of money using the APDs for transporting men back and forth. Another thing, dear, whenever I do get out and am home, I never want to see another sea as long as I live.

—Love to my girls. XXX XXX XXX,
I love you, Short timer, Lou

October 17, at sea

My Dearest One: Well, darling, no doubt by this time you know about the points being dropped As you know I have 42½ points now, so I have enough to get out and when November 1 comes around, I'll have 43¼. I heard all about it tonight over the radio when I was on watch.

Darling, you should have heard me howl when I heard the news. I was so happy inside thinking of you as to how swell you must feel now for it will be just a matter of days and I'll be coming home. Home to stay at last with you and my little girls around me. Oh, my darling, I'm so happy I could cry, but I guess an old salt like me couldn't ever cry anymore. Tell me, dear, as to how you felt when you heard the news? And how did you act?

Oh, darling, I feel so wonderful knowing that I'm getting out for good now...I only hope that I'll be able to get home in time for Christmas to help you dress the tree up for our sweet little girls.

—Love to all of you, Short timer, Lou

October 23, Manila

My Darling Irma: We are taking 150 Navy men to Manus Island, just a little over 1200 miles from here, will take about five days to get there.

Taking these men over there only means one thing. These men will relieve others for Discharge. Am bringing others back to Pearl Harbor or the states. I'll have a swell chance to get off and come back home on another ship.

Hi, darling, just thought I would write another page, for I have some good news to tell you. Our skipper said to my 1st lieutenant this morning that after we take men to Manus Island we will head for home, meaning the good old U.S. Isn't that good news, dear, for that means that once we hit the states it will only be a few days aboard the Bull and I'll be shipped to the discharge center. Once

I am there it will only take 72 hours or less to be discharged. Oh, my dear, if only nothing happens, like changing those orders and staying out here like they do sometimes.

—Love to all, Short timer, Lou

November 3

My Darling Love: Well, dearest, today all I did was to pack my seabag, because I may get off at Samar [island] when we get there tomorrow.

Oh, darling, at last that certain day has come around, all I do now is go around with a smile on my face just thinking of you. Also thinking of those two sweet darlings, little girls of ours. Honestly, dear, now that I know that I am getting out I just can't fall asleep.

We didn't get any mail at Manus Island, it's either at Manus Island or Manila. Hope there is a bunch of them for me because, dear, if I get off the ship I won't get your letters anymore. So when you get this letter do not write to me anymore, it will only be sent back to you. But I will write to you and keep you informed of all the news.

For as soon as we drop anchor, our skipper will go ashore and find out what we are to do, but I'm sure that we will be told to report back to Manila, for that is the home base of all APDs and where they get their orders from.

So now, my darling, dearest, sweets, little woman of mine, I will say Goodnight.

—Love, love to all of you, Short timer, Lou

November 5

Dearest Lou: We are all fine, just waiting for the day when we shall all be together. I am making plans for a wonderful Xmas. I do hope I will not be disappointed.

I had my teeth examined and the dentist estimated the work at $200.00. This is a lot of money, I know. I wasn't even going to mention my teeth to you, but I find I can't pay for it. So I'm asking you if you thought it would be all right if I cashed in our bonds? We have three $50.00 bonds worth a total of $112.50. And we have five $25.00 bonds worth a total of $93.75. Together it will cover the cost of the dentist. What shall I do? I hate to cash the bonds, but my teeth are already started and I want them finished.

Rose and I were talking about how high the prices are. She and her husband feel the pinch too. You know he works at a Bomber Plant and makes maybe $30.00-$35.00 a week. We hope things will get better before you come home so you can get a decent job with decent pay.

The $80.00 I got from you is spent, I think I wrote you just where it went. We have $40.00 in the bank, but we will need that for when you get home. Let me know what you think, as always things like this come up around Xmas and when you are expected home. I get so darn sick of trying to meet expenses and never quite making it. Maybe I'll let you take over when you get home. Maybe you can do better.

—Love, Irma

November 7

Dearest Hubby of Mine: There is really nothing new to write about. Maybe by reading some of your letters over I can answer a few questions.

Darling, it is so wonderful looking at all the men's clothing in the windows. These past two years I always made it a point not to see men's displays. Now I can stop and plan all the things you ought to get. I do hope your green and brown winter suit will fit you. Then we won't need to worry about a suit for you until spring. But you will need a new overcoat and a hat, I think a brown tweed

one would be swell. You'll need a brown hat and shoes to match, besides so many little things. I wonder if any of your shirts will fit.

Darling, darling I can hardly wait to see you in civilian clothes again, so handsome and manly, not like a kid in that Navy suit.

Did you get the birthday card we sent? We sent a couple packages too. We also sent couple packages for Xmas, just candy and stuff, just in case you wouldn't get home.

Gee, hon, hurry home, I've got a burning fever to buy you something. I kept stopping at the tie counter and got away just in time. You never did like any of the ties I picked for you. So I'll wait and we'll buy things together.

—Love—Irma & the girls

November 7, Samar Island

My Darling Irma: I'm so happy, dear, for we are leaving tomorrow morning to board a ship for the states. We came ashore two days ago from our ship, there are 24 of us here in the hut and mud, and there is plenty of mud here.

I figure the ship will take about 18 days to get to the states. I am 7,000 miles away from the states now altogether, dear, from here to you is ten thousand miles. But, my sweet, in a couple of days we will be closer than ever, and as soon as I can I will call you up.

Oh, my dearest, I can hardly wait now to be able to see you again and to kiss you. Dearest, I am so happy I just can't write anymore so the next time you hear from me it will be by phone.

—Love, Lou

Enlisted personnel traveled to one of twenty separation centers across the United States for final discharge. Before receiving a certificate of discharge, all servicemen and women were required to have a medical examination, civilian readjustment counseling if necessary, and information on their rights and benefits as a veteran as specified in the GI Bill. Their rights were outlined in a pamphlet,

"Going Back to Civilian Life," published by the War and Navy Departments in August 1945.

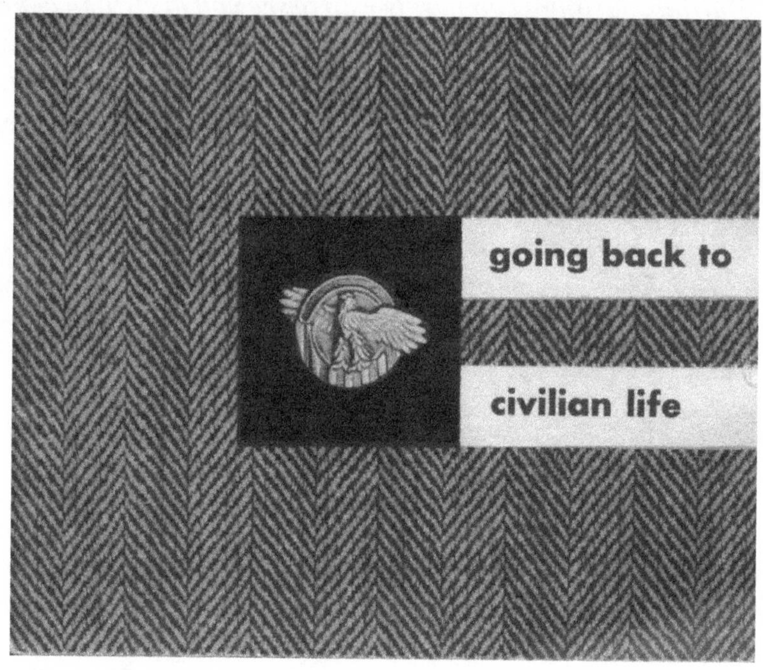

All servicemen and women received this pamphlet when they separated from the military. (1943)

Congress amended the Servicemen's Readjustment Act of 1944 to guarantee education and training for all military personnel up to $500 per year for four years, plus an allowance ranging from $65 to $90 a month. Mustering-out (discharge) pay up to $500 was based on length of service. (Lou received $300). Unemployment insurance was available for 56 weeks at $20 per week, and companies had to provide a job to former employees. The most widely used military benefit was government-backed loans (up to $4,000) for purchasing homes, farms, and businesses.

Soon after his ship docked in California, Lou boarded a train for the Toledo, Ohio, separation center. After his demobilization requirements were met, he left for home, his Honorable Discharge papers, dated December 10, 1945, in hand. He separated from the Navy rated as Coxswain (T) with three battle stars for exemplary service in the Pacific Theater, as well.

Lou arrived in downtown Cleveland by train at the Terminal Tower, the same place he had departed from in 1944. Waiting not so patiently on the station platform was a freshly coiffed Irma and his two daughters in matching outfits sewn by her just for the occasion.

When Irma saw Lou step off the train with his seabag thrown over his shoulder, she let out a whoop and ran to him, the girls trailing behind. As Irma threw her arms around him, Lou dropped his bag and grabbed her and they exchanged a long kiss. They had not kissed in 14 months.

"I'm so glad you're home for good," she sobbed. "And safe. I thought this day would never come. It's been so long."

"I love you so much, hon," he said, his eyes overflowing with tears. "I'm never leaving your side again." He tightened his grip.

"Me either," she said, leaning against him. "We're going to rebuild our lives with the kids."

The girls were clutching her skirt and peering up at the man they had rarely seen and hardly knew. He bent down and swept each of them up for a hug and kiss, his moustache tickling their cheeks.

"Here's my two dolls," he said. "We're finally all together."

After waiting four months for his discharge, they were able to reunite in time to trim the Christmas tree and celebrate his homecoming and the season as a family. It had been two years since they had shared the holidays, and it would be the children's first Christmas with their father. Lou and Irma considered themselves fortunate. He had made it home safe and sound; 400,000 U.S. servicemen and women did not.

Their love had stayed true and strong through their difficult separation, helped by the hundreds of letters they exchanged. It proved to be an important loving connection between home front and battlefront that they built on in the postwar years. Did they ever sit down and reread the letters? We'll never know.

Author's Postscript

May 14,1945, South Pacific

My Dearest Wife: Many are the times I feel you at my side, hon, especially at night on my watches. It is so dark topside that one can just make out the forms of the ships around us, and the sky is studded with stars. Those are the times I feel you by my side with your cheek close to mine, and always feeling you are talking to me. So you see, dear, we are never far apart, for there is a part of us together always. Even when I read your sweet letters, you seem to be talking right to me and laughing in your cute way. When two people are in love such as we, only they can imagine these things and feel them like we do.

—Goodnight, sweetheart, Lou

My father passed away in 2003 at the age of 90, my mother in 2013 when she was 97 years old. Both of them died before I read all of the letters in this book. Together with the photos they vividly bring to life the home front in the 1940s, and the World War II Pacific battlefront.

Like many veterans of World War II, my dad didn't want to talk much about his experiences, and I didn't know the right questions, and, anyway, he was always surprised I wanted to know. I wish I had more information about his life as a child in Budapest and Cleveland. In his letters I finally learned the details of his war years, and the battle scars that resulted in the explosive nightmares he experienced many nights. From my bedroom I could hear his distressed yelling, as my mother tried to shake him awake, shushing him to be quiet. In the letters I also found a father I didn't always recognize growing up, a man who was warm and demonstrative and able to express his feelings of love and yearning. I often wonder what happened to that man. Writing this book has allowed me to rediscover and appreciate some touching moments in our father-daughter relationship.

I also regret I didn't dig more deeply into these letters while my mother was still alive and could fill in the blanks—a lesson to all to capture your family's past while you can. If I knew more about her childhood, I could have more fully understood her life as a second-generation immigrant and war wife. She was a very open, emotional person, and an expressive thinker and writer. If I could have included additional personal experiences, her story would have been even more compelling. Because she was a self-proclaimed romantic, she must have cherished the husband revealed in these letters. I think that's why she carted the box of letters house to house across the country.

Offspring of first-generation immigrants are members of the "Greatest Generation." They changed the face of America—economically, politically, and culturally—through hard work, perseverance, and a strong sense of duty that was instilled by their parents. Neither of my parents ever mentioned that their immigrant background affected their ability to attain the good life in the United States or that they experienced massive discrimination growing up Hungarian in America. Instead my mother railed against big money, the divide between the rich and poor, how the cards were stacked against the lower class. She was a loyal supporter of Franklin D. Roosevelt, and grieved his unexpected death in 1945 as a leader who fought for the "little guy."

While the letters tell a story of love, loneliness, and yearning, they also demonstrate how descriptions of everyday happenings helped to bridge the distance when spouses were in different worlds, trying to hold onto the fabric of former lives. The need to keep their shared life alive, before war intervened and changed everything, was common for all wartime couples. Holding a letter scrawled with ardent declarations of love forever, written on fluttery parchment stationery in pastel tones of baby blue or shell pink, what could be more reminiscent of normal times? What could be more romantic? And my mother loved romances.

Unfortunately, letter writing has fallen out of favor—what a loss. Instead, we rely on emails to communicate even the most personal feelings and events. Somehow emails don't convey the same warm possibilities as letters, and certainly wouldn't be clutched close to the heart or put under a pillow at night.

The family photos from the time period of these love letters also provided clues to the life my parents lived, and an image of the 1940s with a war raging. I was lucky the family photos were saved along with the letters. The black-and-white snapshots of my dad in his sailor suit taken with the ubiquitous Brownie camera seemed to portray happy times. Those of he and my mother radiate the warmth of their love. As is often noted about periods of crisis, life goes on.

Other tangible odds and ends of their war experiences remain: my dad's Navy pea coat and wool watch cap that warmed him through many Cleveland snowstorms; his sailor suit and hat, hanging in my closet; his U.S. Navy bracelet and dog tags in my jewelry box; a copy of the 1940 edition of the naval training bible, *The Bluejackets' Manual,* that I riffled through as a child; and souvenirs he brought back from the Philippines stored in one of the drawers of mom's well-worn Singer sewing machine, now a side table at my house.

As a third-generation American, it's difficult for me to comprehend the everyday difficulties my family faced in building a life and the sacrifices they made to be accepted as Americans. One of the first traditions to disappear in our house while I was growing up was speaking Hungarian. When my sister went to school and had trouble learning English, we were forbidden to speak it. My mother's goal was to be sure our family, and particularly her children, fit into the culture around us.

Immigrant roots and being "just off the boat" increased the challenges for members of all ethnic groups. Well into the second half of the 20th century, immigration laws fueled by the economic hardships of the Great Depression enforced the "great divide" between native born and "those others." My parents' experiences mirror the times today when those seeking asylum to join the melting pot of America might be subject to the same treatment that existed 100 years ago. I find it troubling that some of the identical rhetoric from my parents' generation is still used by many in this country today. Americans, who formed a nation of immigrants, are carrying around a great deal of baggage on this issue that is easily ignited. How and when will we be able to come to terms with it?

The letters and photographs I referenced for this book and the research I have done, have enabled me to see my parents in a new light, as immigrants with many hopes and aspirations that were defined by the immigrant experience. Like other military families, and the nation as a whole, they had to put aside personal wants and lives until V-J Day. It must have been difficult to go from wartime romance to the harsh realities of day-to-day, postwar marital life. The romantic personas created in the letters would be tested by the challenges of adapting from wartime to peacetime and would begin to change shape.

I have come to the realization that I shied away from my ethnic background as I was growing up, finishing high school and college, and starting a family, not acknowledging its important influence in my life. Was I worried that I could become an outsider in my social groups because of it? Did my grandmother's use of broken English set me apart from my non-ethnic friends? I see now I was a product of my generation, and those before me, when non-Northern European immigrants were not especially welcome. It wasn't until the Age of Aquarius in the 1960s that one's ethnicity was valued and celebrated, providing an opportunity to build on one's nationality to the benefit of self and society. I carry some guilt and sadness that it has taken me so long to appreciate my roots. Writing this book is an affirmation of those feelings. I have much to be thankful for in my immigrant upbringing, especially the Hungarian traditions and customs that have enriched my life over the years. As I think about my childhood, I see the strong ethnic roots that were planted and how they have served me all my life.

The most amazing outcomes in my family? A mere ten years after the war ended, my parents were able to build a modern house in the suburbs (with the help of the GI Bill, I presume). When she was in her 70s, my mother went back to school to earn the high school degree denied by her Darvas Fashion School experience and then went on to earn an associate's degree in business administration at the local community college. She made sure my sister and I both earned college degrees and she paid the bill.

I wrote this book to share the beautiful love letters my parents wrote, to depict the views of a home front wife and a battlefront husband. It soon became apparent to me that this was the nation's story too. The war wives of World War II were a unique occurrence in our country's history—the first time women served in the military and worked in factories. Home front moms have taken a backseat to Rosie the Riveter and servicewomen in our nation's consciousness. I hope this book helps to set the record straight.

War wives didn't know that the life they led during the war would influence the role of women in society in the decades ahead. Women like my mother thought they were just doing their job, raising the kids and running a household, not creating a major societal change for their gender. Max Lerner, well-known educator and journalist believed that "When the classic work on the history of women comes to be written, the biggest force for change in their lives will turn out to have been war. Curiously, war produces more dislocations in the lives of women who stay home than of men who go off to fight."

The lives of war wives would prove to be a catalyst for many future social changes, especially a feminist liberation movement that increased women's lifestyle choices, access to college degrees, and opportunities to climb the business ladder and break the glass ceiling.

The red thread running through this book, of course, is the letters. They have revealed a great deal about my mom and dad, and what a loving marriage can be in wartime. They have also provided a comforting and healing road to travel following my mother's death. Touched by the letters and intrigued with the parents I found, I wanted to share this loving wartime romance that is a universal story for wartime wives. I only wish they were here to read their story. I think they would be pleased.

Acknowledgements

I've been writing this book since 2014. In that time, many have contributed to its successful completion. My husband provides continual support and is my #1 cheerleader.

My daughter Heather is always supportive in so many ways. Both she and her brother Nathan believed in this story about their grandparents and was glad it could be shared. My friend Mary's mother served in the U.S. Army as a WAC code-breaker and we have traded stories.

We should all be grateful for our country's research institutions: the Library of Congress, National Archives, and the Ellis Island Museum of Immigration, all an author's best friends. (If you haven't visited Ellis Island, do so. Many in this country have family that passed through Ellis Island and helped build the country we are today.) I am also grateful for the Cleveland Memory Project at Cleveland State University, and the Sedona Public library and its reference librarians.

Many to thank have passed on. Most notable among them was Barb, a friend for fifty years. She always believed in my writings, and was suitably impressed that I was a published author. She read parts of this book, and was waiting for its completion. I think she would have loved it, she was such a romantic.

My sister Lola has been gone almost twenty years so she wasn't aware of the letters or the planned book. She plays a feature role in the letters so it is sad she will never read it.

An author learns from other authors and editors and the many writing workshops they attend. So here's to all the authors whose brains I picked to make this a better book.

About the Author

Born and raised in Cleveland, Ohio, Diane Phelps Budden spent over 30 years in corporate and academic marketing in Michigan before moving to Sedona, Arizona, and launching Red Rock Mountain Press. She wrote and published the picture book *Shade; a story about a very smart raven,* followed by *The Author's Concise Guide to Marketing: how to jumpstart sales of your self-published book* for first-time authors needing marketing skills. Responding to the need for a non-fiction book about ravens for middle grade children, as well as adult raven lovers, she researched and wrote *The Un-Common Raven: one smart bird* that received recognition as a Panelist Pick in the 2013 Southwest Books of the Year and a finalist in the New Mexico-Arizona Book Awards. She travels the state to give programs and workshops on ravens, self-publishing, and creative writing. She also works in clay sculpture, predominately figurative pieces.

Contact the author at www.dianephelpsbudden.com.

Source Notes

Introduction

The story of my parents and their letters….: U.S. Department of the Interior. National Park Service, *World War II and the American Home Front*, p. 58.

"Rosie the Riveter" became the icon….: Campbell, *Women at War with America*, p. 10.

"Oh, I was just a housewife….": Ibid., p. 7.

Chapter 1—1930s: An Immigrant Grows Up in the Great Depression

They had joined an unprecedented….: Mindell, *Ethnic Families in America*, p. 17.

The 1920 U.S. Census counted 945,801 persons….: U.S. Bureau of the Census, *Historical Statistics of the United States*, 1789-1945, p. 33.

A few years later the Immigration….: Israelowitz, *Ellis Island Guide*, p. 27.

Getting to her new country….: Ibid., p. 11.

Steerage tickets might cost….: Ibid., p. 11.

When Lila moved to Cleveland….: Papp, *Hungarian Americans and Their Communities of Cleveland*, p. 232.

By 1920 Hungarians made up….: Ibid., p. 234.

Immigrant groups coming to America….: Morrison, *American Mosaics*, p. 59.

When Irma was old enough, mother and daughter….: Lewis, *To Market, To Market*, p. 12.

Irma's generation was part of a new….: Schrum, *Some Wore Bobby Sox*, p.12.

She made a green cotton pique….Secrest, *Elsa Schiaparelli*, p. 137.

In 1932, 23.6 per cent of the workforce….: U.S. Department of Labor. *U.S. Bureau of Labor Statistics*, p. 15.

Irma and her friends volunteered….: Western Reserve Historical Society. "West Side Community House, 1900-1970." http://norton.wrhs.org/collections/view?docId=ead/PG336.xml;query=;brand=def

As the summer began to fade, Irma…..: Air Racing History, Cleveland Air Races. http://www.airracinghistory.freeola.com/Cleveland%20Air%20Races.htm.

Chapter 2—1940s: The Newlyweds

His name was listed on the passenger….www.libertyellisfoundation, passenger manifest list #22.

Causing a chain migration….: Cleveland State University. "History of Hungarian-Americans in Cleveland." http://www.clevelandmemory.org/hungarian/hhac.html.

Lou's father was able to obtain a job….; Case Western Reserve. The Encyclopedia of Cleveland History. "Jones and Laughlin Steel Corp." http://ech.case.edu/cgi/article.pl?id=JALSC.

Lou's family was lucky they immigrated before….: Werner, *Passage to America*, p. 163.

A law passed in 1924 reduced quotas further….: Ibid., p. 163.

On the 1940 Federal census Lou….: U.S. Bureau of the Census, *Historical Statistics of the United States, 1789-1945*, p. 33.

By 1940, movie attendance had increased….Brown, *Movie Time, p. 153.*

The fair covered over 1200 acres….: *Official Guide Book*, p. 6+.

"The World of Fashion is out to prove….": Ibid., p. 43.

They ate lunch at the Hungary pavilion ….: *World's Fair Daily*, August 22, 1940.

Printmakers were using lithography or etching….: *Official Guide Book*, p. 13.

An April 1,1942, article in *Vogue* magazine….: *Vogue*, April 1, 1942, p. 75.

Cleveland reacted as much of the country….: Albrecht, *Cleveland in World War II*, p. 180.

Chapter 3—1943: Boot Camp Blues

Congress had established the first peacetime….: U.S. Department of the Interior. National Park Service, *World War II and the American Home Front*, p. 58.

Typical hat styles of the Forties….: Sessions. vintagedancer. com/?s=1940s+hats.

Hats were equally important for the….: Steinberg, *Hatless Jack*, p. 60.

Like other housewives, Irma's favorite radio shows….: Sickels, *The 1940s*, p. 214.

When World War II began, the radio was….: Lingeman, *Don't You Know There's a War On?,* p. 223.

From 1933 to 1945, President Franklin D. Roosevelt….: Sickels, *The 1940s*, p. 188.

According to the U.S. Bureau of Labor Statistics….: U.S. Department of Labor, *U.S. Bureau of Labor Statistics,* p. 15.

A civilian rationing program was….: Weatherford, *Americans and World War II*, p. 201.

A point system for rationing…." Sickels, *The 1940s*, p. 101.

Once the war started the shortage of suitable fabrics….: Ibid., p. 80.

Congress had passed a law in December….: National Park Service, *World War II and the American Home Front*, p. 58.

Chapter 4—1944: Daddy All Gone

Lou's orders were to join….: Division of Naval History, Ships Histories Section, p. 1.

According to the Division of Naval History….: Ibid., p. 1.

The Office of War Information….: Campbell, *Women at War With America*, p. 72.

The Servicemen's Dependents Allowance Act….: Grossman, *Cornell Law Review*, p.217.

Starting pay for servicemen of all branches of the….: Tillit, *Barron's National Business and Financial Weekly,* April 24, 1944. http://www.usmm.org/barrons.html.

Censorship of mail was intended to….: PBS American Experience, "Censorship." http://www.pbs.org/wgbh/american

On July 28, the *Bull* was reassigned….: U.S. Navy, History of USS *Bull*, p. 2.

Starting in the 1930s, shopping in downtown….: Klein, Let's Go Shopping at the Square, p. 28.

Sterling & Welch, the oldest of all the stores….: Faircloth, *Images of America: Cleveland's Department Stores*, p. 14.

Chapter 5—1945, Winter: Miss You So Much

In Pearl Harbor, the Bull's orders were to board members….: Flynn, http://militaryhonors.sid-hill.us/mil/uidt14.htm.

V-Mail or Victory Mail was developed by….: Smithsonian National Postal Museum, http://library.si.edu/libraries/national-postal-museum-library.

To finance the military operations of the most expensive….: United States History, World War II Rationing. http://www.u-s-history.com/pages/h1674.html.

In the 1940s, motion pictures, along with radio….: Sickels, *The 1940s*, p. 200.

Every battle in the Pacific War was crucial….: Gow, *Okinawa 1945*, p. 22.

Okinawa was invaded on April 1….: Ibid., p. 71.

When the island was finally captured on March….: Doyle, *World War II in Numbers*, p. 100+.

Chapter 6—1945, Spring: When Will It All End?

A number of studies conducted shortly after the war….: Duvall, "Loneliness and the Serviceman's Wife," *Marriage and Family Living*, pp. 77-81.

The Bull's Log Book recounts their role as….: U.S. National Archives, Records Administration, USN Deck log, *USS Bull*, April 1945.

One war wife cleverly created….: Gurfein, Library of Congress, www.American Folklife Center.

Chapter 7—1945, Fall: The Home Stretch

The Japanese surrendered on August 15, 1945….: National World War II Museum, "V-J Day,"https://www.nationalww2museum.org/war/articles/v-j-day.

The immediacy of the moment was captured forever….: *Reminisce*, pp. 8-30.

Elwood Dehority of Howe, Indiana, shared his memory….: Ibid., p. 8+.

Another New Yorker remembered that on …." Ibid., p. 8+.

Not be outdone by New Yorkers….: Albrecht, *Cleveland in World War II*, p. 188.

Soon after the Japanese surrendered, America's Armed….: U.S. Department of the Navy, *All Hands*, p. 12+.

In order to be considered for discharge or separation….: Ibid., p. 64+.

"Where is the war wife who only the other day…": Millet, *Cleveland Plain Dealer,* September 1, 1945.

Enlisted personnel traveled to one of twenty….: U.S. Department of the Navy, *All Hands*, 12+.

Congress amended the Servicemen's Adjustment Act….: Humes, *Over Here*, p. 29.

400,000 servicemen and women had died….: National Park Service, *World War II and the American Home Front,* p. 59.

Author's Postscript

Max Lerner, well-known educator and journalist….: *Public Journal: Marginal Notes on Wartime America,* p.19.

Bibliography

A+E Networks Corps. HISTORY.com. *November 11: This Day in History, World War II, 1942: Draft Age is Lowered to18.* http://www.history.com/this-day-in-history/draft-age-is-lowered-to-18.

Air Racing History, "Cleveland Air Races." http://www.airracing-history.freeola.com/Cleveland%20Air%20Races.htm.

Albrecht, Brian, and James Banks. *Cleveland in World War II.* Charleston, SC: The History Press, 2015.

Altschuler, Glenn and Stuart Blumin. *Pivotal Moment in American History: GI Bill: The New Deal for Veterans.* Cary GB: Oxford 2009. ProQuest Ebrary: Web 29, December 2016.

Anderson, Karen. *Wartime Women: Sex Roles, Family Relations, and the Status of Women During World War II.* Westport, Connecticut: Greenwood Press, 1981.

Brokaw, Tom. *The Greatest Generation.* New York: Random House, 1998.

Brown, Gene. *Movie Time: a Chronology of Hollywood and the Movie Industry from its Beginnings to the Present*. New York: Macmillan, 1995.

Campbell, D'Ann. *Women at War with America: Private Lives in a Patriotic Era*. Cambridge, Massachusetts: Harvard University Press, 1984.

Case Western Reserve. The Encyclopedia of Cleveland History. "Hungarians." http://ech.case.edu/. —"Jones and Laughlin Steel Corp." http://ech.case.edu/.

Cleveland State University. The Cleveland Memory Project. "History of Hungarian-Americans In Cleveland." http://www.clevelandmemory.org/hungarian/hhac.html.

Cunningham, Chet. *The Frogmen of World War II*. New York, NY: Simon & Schuster, Inc., 2005.

Davis, Maxine. "Women Without Men," *Good Housekeeping*, March 1942, 114: 30, 180-181, http://hearth.library.cornell.edu/cgi/t/text/pageviewer-idx?c=hearth;rgn=%20text;idno=6417403_1371_003;view=image;seq=32.

Destroyer History Foundation, Destroyer Escorts. http://destroyer-history.org/de/.

Doyle, Peter. *World War II in Numbers: an Infographic Guide to the Conflict, its Conduct, and its Casualties*. Buffalo, NY: Firefly Books, Inc., 2013.

Duvall, Evelyn Millis. "Loneliness and the Serviceman's Wife." National Conference on Family Relations. *Marriage and Family Living*, November 1945: 77-81.

Ellis Island Foundation. "Passenger Manifest List." April 30, 1921, #22, Lasslo Vajda.

Faircloth, Christopher. *Images of America: Cleveland's Department Stores.* Charleston, SC: Arcadia Publishing, 2009.

Flynn, Joe, ed. "The History of Underwater Demolition Team 14, As Told by the Men Who Lived it." http://militaryhonors.sid-hill.us/mil/udt14.htm.

Foster, Simon. *US Navy Casualties from Okinawa 1945: Final Assault on the Empire*. London, UK: Arms and Armor Press, 1994.

Gow, Ian. *Okinawa 1945: Gateway to Japan.* Garden City, NY: Doubleday & Company, 1985.

Grasmehr, Paul, Pritzker Military Museum & Library. U.S. Military Deaths at Okinawa. Email message to author, June 10, 2015.

Grossman, Harry. "Administration of Family Allowances for Men in Military Service." *Cornell Law Review* 29, November 1943: 217. http://scholarship.law.cornell.edu/cgi/viewcontent.cgi?article=4595&context=clr.

Gurfein, Marion. "Goofy Gremlins." Library of Congress, American Folklife Center, Veterans History Project, 1942.

Harris, Kristina. *Vintage Fashions for Women: 1920s-1940s.* Atglen, PA: Schiffer Publishing Ltd., 1996.

Humes, Edward. *Over Here: How the G.I. Bill Transformed the American Dream*. New York, NY: Harcourt, Inc., 2006.

Israelowitz, Oscar. *Ellis Island Guide with Lower Manhattan.* Brooklyn, NY: Israelowitz Publishing, 1990.

Klein, Richard. *Let's Go Shopping at the Square, Cleveland's Leading Downtown Department Stores: a Business Legacy.* Cleveland State University: The Cleveland Memory Project, 2014. http://images.ulib.csuohio.edu/cdm/singleitem/collection/general/id/7367/rec/1.

Lerner, Max. *Public Journal: Marginal Notes on Wartime America.* New York: The Viking Press. 1945.

Lewis, Joanne M. *To Market, To Market: an Old-fashioned Family Story: the West Side Market.* Cleveland Heights, OH: Elandon Books, Inc., 1881.

Lingeman, Richard R. *Don't You Know There's a War On?: the American Home Front, 1941-45.* New York: G.P. Putnam's Sons, 1970.

Litoff, Judy Barrett, David C. Smith, Barbara Wooddall Taylor, and Charles E. Taylor. *MissYou: the World War II letters of Barbara Wooddall Taylor and Charles E. Taylor*. Athens, Georgia: The University of Georgia Press, 1990.

Litoff, Judy Barrett. *Since You Went Away: World War II Letters from American Women on the Home Front*. Lawrence, Kansas: University Press of Kansas, 1991.

Millet, Ruth. "All's Rosy Now in the Service Wife's World." *The Cleveland Plain Dealer*, September 1, 1945.

Mindel, Charles H., Robert Habenstein, and Roosevelt W. Wright. *Ethnic Patterns and Variations*; fourth edition. Upper Saddle River, NJ: Prentice Hall, 1998.

Morrison, Joan, and Charlotte Fox Zabusky. *American Mosaic: the Immigrant Experience Words of Those Who Lived It.* New York: E.P. Dutton, 1980.

The National World War II Museum. "Iwo Jima Fact Sheet." New Orleans, LA, http://www.nationalww2museum.org/focus-on/iwo-jima-fact-sheet.pdf.—"V-J Day." https://www.nationalww2museum.org/war/articles/v-j-day.

NavSource Naval History. Amphibious Photo Archive, USS Bull (APD-78). http://www.navsource.org/archives/10/04/04.

Official Guide Book: The World's Fair of 1940 in New York, For Peace and Freedom. New York, NY: Rogers, Kellogg, Stillson, Inc., 1940.

PBS American Experience. "Censorship." http://www.pbs.org/wgbh/american experience/features/general-article/warletters- censorship/.

Papp, Susan. *Hungarian Americans and Their Communities of Cleveland.* Cleveland Ethnic Heritage Studies series, Cleveland State University, 1981. http://www.clevelandmemory.org/hungarians/.

Reminisce. "A Time to Remember: Moments that Shaped Us, War is over!" June/July 2015: 8-30.

Sabol, John T. *Cleveland's Buckeye Neighborhood (Image of America Series).* Charleston, SC: Arcadia Publishing, 2011.

Schrum, Kelly. *Some Wore Bobby Sox: The Emergence of Teenage Girls' Culture, 1920-1945*. New York, NY: Palgrave Macmillan, 2004.

Secrest, Meryle. *Elsa Schiaparelli*. New York, NY: Alfred A. Knopf, 2014.

Sessions, Debbie. "1940s Hats History." Vintage Dancer, vintage-dancer.com/?s=1940s+hats.

Sickels, Robert. *The 1940s*. Westport, CT: Greenwood Press, 2004.

Smithsonian National Postal Museum. http://library.si.edu/libraries/national-postal-museum-library

Steinberg, Neil. *Hatless Jack: the President, the Fedora, and the History of an American Style.* New York, NY: Penguin Group, 2004.

Tillitt, Malvern Hall. "Army-Navy Pay Tops Most Civilians;' Unmarried Private's Income Equivalent to $3,600 Salary." *Barron's National Business and Financial Weekly,* April 24, 1944, http://www.usmm.org/barrons.html.

U.S. Bureau of the Census. *Historical Statistics of the United States, 1789-1945*, Washington D.C., 1949.

U.S. Department of the Interior. National Parks Service. National Historic Landmarks Program. *World War II and the American Home Front*. Washington DC, October 2007.

U.S. Department of Labor. U.S. Department of Labor Statistics. 100 Years of U.S. Consumer Spending: Data for the Nation,

New York City, and Boston Data. August 3, 2006. www.bls.gov/opub/uscs/report991.pdf.

U.S. Department of Labor. Bureau of Labor Statistics. Cost of Clothing for Moderate-Income Families, 1935-44. Bulletin No. 789, from the *Monthly Labor Review*, July 1944.

U.S. Department of Labor. Bureau of Labor Statistics. Retail prices: Food and Coal. January 1941 and Year 1940. Washington DC: GPO.

U.S. Department of the Navy. Bureau of Naval Personnel Information Bulletin. "Information for Dischargees." *All Hands*, November 1945: 12-15. http://www.navy.mil/ah_online/archpdf/ah194511.pdf.—"Navy Demobilization: Point Score Cut." *All Hands*, November 1945: 64-67. http://www.navy.mil/ah_online/archpdf/ah194511.pdf.

U.S. National Archives. USN Deck Log Book of the U.S.S. Bull, APD 78, March 1-April 30, 1945.

U.S. National Archives. National Personnel Records Center. Military Records for Louis Steve Vajda. http://www.archives.gov/veterans/military-service-records/.

U.S. Navy Division of Naval History. "History of USS Bull (APD78)," 1953:2.www.nhhc_foia@navy.mil.

United States History. "World War II Rationing." http://www.u-s-history.com/pages/h1674.html.

United States History. "U.S. War Bonds," http://www.u-s-history.com/pages/h1682.html.

Vogue. "A Primer on Pants," April 1, 1942, p. 75.

Weatherford, Doris. *American Women and World War II*. New York: Facts On File, 1990.

Werner, Emmy E. *Passage to America: Oral Histories of Child Immigrants from Ellis Island and Angel Island*. Washington, DC: Potomac Books, Inc., 2009.

Western Reserve Historical Society. "West Side Community House, 1900-1970." http://norton.wrhs.org/collections/view?docId=ead/PG336.xml;query=;brand=default

Yellin, Emily. *Our Mother's War: American Women at Home and at the Front During World War II*. New York, NY: Free Press, 2004.